I0467750

CLIFF CLARIFIES BUSINESS GROWTH

By

CLIFF HARDCASTLE
OBE FIET

To my wife, friends and work colleagues who helped me through the bad patches.

CONTENTS

INTRODUCTION 1

1. THE SEVEN STAGES OF COMPANY GROWTH 3

   WHY GROW? WHAT ARE THE ALTERNATIVES? 6

2. PEOPLE ARE THE ESSENTIAL FUEL................................9

   1. WHY ARE PEOPLE SO IMPORTANT? 9
   2. HOW TO RECRUIT, TRAIN, MOTIVATE, AND REWARD NEW
      STAFF.. 10
   3. RECRUITING ISSUES 11
   4. HOW TO RECRUIT.. 12
   5. HOW TO TRAIN STAFF.. 15
   6. MOTIVATION... 16
   7. IF YOU 'SPIN', EMPLOYEES WILL KNOW 16
   8. DIRECT REGULAR CONTACT BETWEEN MANAGERS AND
      STAFF.. 20

3. SEVEN CORPORATE OBJECTIVES 22

   1. CONTINUITY.. 23
   2. PROFIT... 23
   3. CUSTOMERS... 24
   4. GROWTH... 24
   5. OUR PEOPLE 25
   6. MANAGEMENT 26
   7. CITIZENSHIP.. 26

4. THE IMPORTANCE OF STRUCTURE...............................28

   1. SOME IDEAS 28
   2. TWO MAIN STRUCTURES AND THEIR CHARACTERISTICS 28
   3. BUSINESS PLANS.. 29
   4. PEOPLE VERSUS STRUCTURE 30
   5. RESPECT FOR OTHERS 31
   6. SYSTEM.. 32
   7. LEADERSHIP 33

8. MANAGERS' RESPONSIBILITY FOR THEIR OWN STAFF........... 33
9. TRUST AND LEADERSHIP... 34
10. COMPANY REPORTING STRUCTURES 35
11. THE HIERARCHICAL TOP-DOWN PYRAMID STYLE
    MANAGEMENT STRUCTURE 36
12. UNDERSTANDING AND GROWING PRIVATE COMPANIES
    AND EMPLOYMENT.. 37

5. THE THREE MAIN WORK PLACES 40

1. UNDERSTANDING YOUR CUSTOMERS' STRUCTURE TO
   INCREASE SALES 40
2. THE PRIVATE SECTOR.. 41
3. THE PUBLIC SECTOR 43
4. THE CHARITABLE/VOLUNTARY SECTOR..................................... 44

6. THE PEOPLE WHO INFLUENCE A COMPANY'S
PERFORMANCE 46

1. SHAREHOLDERS/OWNERS.. 46
2. THE BOARD OF DIRECTORS 50
3. BOARD STRUCTURE.. 51
4. THE ROLE OF THE DIRECTORS.. 52
5. GOOD AGENDAS HELP GROWTH 53
6. SMALLER COMPANIES 54
7. THE MANAGERS... 56
8. THE EMPLOYEES 59
9. THE CUSTOMERS.. 62
10. THE SUPPLIERS 64

7. PEOPLE MANAGEMENT 67

1. HOW TO MANAGE DIVERSE PEOPLE 67
2. TO GROW SAFELY THE SENIOR STAFF MUST REGULARLY
   MEET WITH PEOPLE THEY ARE RESPONSIBLE FOR................. 70
3. AN EXAMPLE OF BAD PRACTICE... 71
4. HOW TO PRUNE INEFFECTIVE PEOPLE... 72

8. GROWTH THROUGH PRODUCT CHOICE AND
DEVELOPMENT..75

1. FORECASTING... 77
2. WAYS FORWARD 79
3. INCREASE INTELLECTUAL PROPERTY (R&D) 87
4. PATENTS.. 88
5. COPYRIGHT.. 89
6. TRADEMARKS.. 91

7. INDUSTRIAL DESIGN 91
8. TRADE DRESS AND TRADE SECRETS 91

9. OTHER GROWTH CREATORS 93

1. SELL MORE TO EXISTING CUSTOMERS! 93
2. ATTRACT NEW CUSTOMERS 94
3. EXPAND YOUR GEOGRAPHIC SALES AREA 96
4. ACQUIRE A NEW PRODUCT RANGE BY BUYING ONE FROM
   ANOTHER COMPANY 100
5. ACQUIRING AN EXISTING COMPANY 101
6. HOW WE GOT A HIGH PRICE IN SELLING RBS 103
7. MISTAKES AND FAILURE IN ACQUISITIONS 106
8. MERGE WITH ANOTHER COMPANY 109
9. MARKET RESEARCH IDEAS 113
10. MARKET RESEARCH LESSONS 116
11. GROW GEOGRAPHICALLY 117

10. UNDERSTAND YOUR RESOURCES 119

SUMMARY OF THE MAIN RESOURCES 119

11. THE TWO TYPES OF CAPITAL 125

1. FIXED CAPITAL AND WORKING CAPITAL 125
2. HOW TO VALUE YOUR COMPANY TO ATTRACT INVESTMENT
   128
3. FINANCIAL PLANNING 130
4. CREDIT RATINGS 132
5. LOANS 133
6. INCREASE OR DECREASE SUPPLIERS 134
7. SOLE SUPPLIER 135
8. AN EXAMPLE OF JAPANESE COMPETITION 135

12. FORECASTING SALES AND FINANCIAL PLANNING
.... 139

1. SAFER FORECASTING 140
2. USING SALES FORECAST IN FINANCIAL FORECASTING 141

13. TAX ISSUES 144

14. WHAT GETS IN THE WAY OF GROWTH? 146

1. COMPETITION 146
2. OPTIMISM 147
3. FEAR OF CHANGE 149
4. POOR OR DISORGANISED MANAGEMENT 150

5. BANKS...152
6. THE GOVERNMENT 154

15. YOUR ABILITIES MUST BE SUITABLE 155

1. PROJECTING AMBITIONS FOR ALL STAFF...................................156
2. BE ARTICULATE AND BELIEVABLE 156
3. BIG LESSONS - TRUST OTHERS CAREFULLY................................158
4. TRUST YOURSELF 158
5. DO WHAT YOU SAY YOU WILL DO 159
6. MANAGEMENT TEAMS 159

ADDENDUM 1... 162

1. INDEX TO ADDENDUM...163
2. REPORTING PROCEDURES TO BE USED......................................167
3. SUMMARY OF AUTHORISATION LEVELS.....................................169
4. DIRECTOR LEVEL SIGNATORY POWERS 171
5. OVERHEAD COSTS..173
6. COMPETENCIES FOR POTENTIAL SENIOR MANAGEMENT..177
7. THE ROLE OF THE WORLDWIDE PRODUCT MANAGER.........180
8. THE ROLE OF A SALES MANAGER..182
9. THE ROLE OF MANAGING DIRECTOR OF A SALES COMPANY
....185
10. RECRUITMENT AND PEOPLE MANAGEMENT POLICIES......187
11. REQUIREMENTS FOR MEMBERS OF THE MAIN BOARD 188
12. GUIDELINES FOR TRADING COMPANIES 189
13. TERMS AND CONDITIONS FOR CONTRACTUAL SALES 192
14. CONTRACT TERMS FOR SCHEDULED ORDERS........................193
15. RULES FOR MANUFACTURING COMPANIES 195
16. MANUFACTURING UNITS IDEAL RATIOS FOR OVERHEAD 200
17. SALES ACTIVITIES 201
18. LIST OF INFORMATION NEEDED FOR LARGER ENQUIRIES
....204
19. FINANCIAL ISSUES 206
   1. TREASURY POLICIES 206
   2. CURRENCY EXPOSURE POLICY.......................................207
   3. STAFF PROCEDURES..207
   4. CURRENCY EXPOSURE MANAGEMENT 213
   5. CREDIT EXPOSURE 218

ADDENDUM 2... 219

1. PRODUCT KNOWLEDGE FOR SALES STAFF 219
2. SALES AREA KNOWLEDGE 220
3. COMPANY KNOWLEDGE...220

4. HOW TO ORGANISE A SALESPERSON'S WORKING DAY....... 221
5. IN FRONT OF A CUSTOMER 223
6. EXPLOITATION OF EXISTING CUSTOMERS 224
7. EXPLOITATION OF A CONTACT WITHIN A COMPANY 224
8. FOLLOW-UP QUOTATIONS AND LITERATURE REQUESTS .. 225
9. REFERENCE SELLING... 225
10. CREATING TARGETS. SET TARGETS AND MEET THEM...... 226
11. ONLINE AND INDIRECT SELLING 226

ACKNOWLEDGMENTS

To all the worldwide staff at Densitron and professionals who advised us. A special word for Alan Rawlins who was instrumental in helping me float Densitron in 1986 and got little thanks at the time.

INTRODUCTION

This book is intended for those business people who have a company that is firmly established and profitable. It provides a good income for the owners, managers and staff including proper provisions for pensions etc., all without working excessive hours. Hopefully it has sufficient after-tax income to allow a consideration of what the future can be.

HOW TO USE THIS BOOK

Whereas starting a company tends to depend upon a relatively well defined set of principles, growth is very much more random. Growth depends very much on the leaders of the company to make intelligent plans based upon an often confusing range of opportunities. Sometimes growth tends to 'just happen', but it still needs managing and controlling. Successful company growth results from the senior leaders or managers having a degree of alertness to opportunity coupled with a firm understanding of business management. Uncontrolled growth is as dangerous as uncontrolled decline – they both lead to bankruptcy.

This book is not written like a novel with a beginning, middle, and end. It is written as a series of interlinked and mutually supportive sections. There is a certain amount of repetition where a given subject is looked at from different angles.

To get the most advantage from its contents I suggest that you identify an aspect of growth that interests you and use the index to identify where this is dealt with in the text.

You can alternatively browse through it, stopping where something interests you. Growing a business is a complex process and is handled differently by different people. At the end of the day you will have to find your own route to success. This book is a reference manual of good practice with examples, but does also deal with danger and failure.

I have added two very useful addenda, one on *reporting procedures* and *controls*, the other concerning *selling*. These are taken from real life situations. They are not recommended as mandatory but once again can be a useful template for you to guide your own thought.

My companion book **'Cliff Clarifies the Business Basics'** can offer a great deal of supporting knowledge.

1. THE SEVEN STAGES OF COMPANY GROWTH

STAGE 1

Understand and define the company as it is at present.

What does the company do?

Who are its customers?

Where are they?

Is it growing? Stable? Or declining?

What is the management structure?

STAGE 2

What are your ambitions?

Think forward by 3 and 5 years and describe the company you want to be.

Do this for sales, profit, employees, location, marketplace, your involvement and position, etc.

STAGE 3

Analyse the present position with reference to your future ambitions.

Check:

Products and services, employees, premises, plant and machinery, management structure.

Marketplace, profitability and gross margin, overhead costs, cash requirements, net worth.

Realisable value, sales processes, production methods and processes, capital needs.

Return on shareholders' funds, return on all capital.

Are you growing, stable, or dying?

STAGE 4

Start the process of change,

Analyse for good and bad practice and list under two headings,

Change the bad things by:

Brainstorming, lateral thinking, backward thinking, research, get advice and ask others.

Ask customers and suppliers.

Carry out continuous development, ask employees.

Use consultants or advisers cautiously.

STAGE 5

Be prepared to welcome and accept change.

Make change a continuing process. Remember there are many routes, many small steps,

Try to maintain evolution rather than revolution. Be prepared to go backwards sometimes, and sideways regularly, in order to go forward.

STAGE 6

Check whether your plans are working.

Measure sales volume, employee number and capability, net worth, profit.

STAGE 7

If it worked do it again. Remembering that if you have changed, so has the rest of the world.

Relaxing is not an option.

WHY GROW?

WHAT ARE THE ALTERNATIVES?

The plain truth is that if a company fails to grow it will be in danger of serious decline and maybe failure. The very least growth required is to be more than inflation.

Recently inflation has not been a big factor for business, but even in the recent past has been a potent challenge in Great Britain when it rose to around 25% per annum in 1976.

In other countries such as Germany it had historically reached even more destructive levels and probably created the seeds of the Second World War.

I had started my new company in February 1972 and inflation reached a peak of 25% in 1975, only falling back to around 5% in the mid-eighties. It was a very confusing time and I can't pretend to remember all the details. We grew strongly throughout that time but it took a very flexible approach and considerable financial agility. Inflation in England was to varying extents mirrored in other countries. This influenced the currency exchange rate between countries which altered the prices of goods that we sold or bought internationally. We used such mechanisms as buying any foreign currency we needed at the same time as we placed orders for new goods or accepted orders from customers.

You can imagine that before the widespread use of computers, ordinary calculators ran hot. Even during and after flotation in 1986 currency exchange rates were worryingly variable. We had expected the £ and $ to reach parity and made many of our financial forecasts on this basis.

However, the £ recovered strongly, making our USA profits decline by around 20% thus putting our flotation in some jeopardy. I can remember my partner in America ringing me at home almost every night in a panic about what was to happen. Needless to say we got through it, 'just'. Being headquartered in London became a great asset. Our banks have recently been vilified in the press and on television but with their incredible expertise on many occasions, including this inflationary period, they became our saviours.

They introduced us to so many financial products that allowed us to trade in relative safety. As an example, we could buy foreign currency in advance but only pay for it when used. Further, we could take options to purchase currency in the future at a given price but only exercise the option if suitable at the time needed. My advice is to research bank facilities at the highest level you can. Your local high street branch will not have the expertise to deal with such complexities.

One huge factor in trying to deal with inflationary matters is staff salaries. Our staff were experiencing increased prices for food and other essentials. They expected us to be able to increase their salaries by inflation plus an extra amount for career progression.

We managed to do all that and still grow strongly throughout this complex period. The need to grow by at least inflation is, I hope, explained somewhat by the stories given above. However, just staying with inflation is a small ambition. Of much greater importance is the effect of aggressive competition. This can come at you in a variety of ways. They may introduce new and better products. They may cut prices either on an ad hoc basis or as the result of improved production techniques. You can only really counter these attacks by trying to grow strongly yourself.

Growth will invigorate your staff and organisation. It will impress shareholders or partners. It will help your company survive an uncertain future. But most of all it should make you richer, which is rarely a bad thing.

2. PEOPLE ARE THE ESSENTIAL FUEL

1. WHY ARE PEOPLE SO IMPORTANT?

When you start your business you are probably alone, although for many ventures there is a rapid need for more help. This will probably be in the nature of office staff and bookkeeping. Recruitment at this vital stage is done by the founder and as was the case with my company, I relied on people I knew; particularly my wife. As the early business is closely run by the founder, the quality of these early people does not always need to be outstanding and the business can rely on the abilities of the founder to help and guide actions.

Referring again to my own experiences, I was very lucky in that the first three people that joined me were so capable that they stayed with me all the way to my retirement. The first two were part-time women office staff who my wife recruited at the local primary school as parents chatted together after delivering their children. They were highly capable and well trained. They were taking time out to raise a family and loved the flexible part-time work that I offered. They remained part-time to the end and shared my workload very intelligently, one eventually becoming a director of the public company we grew into.

From these early closely monitored staff there is a need to match the company's growth with a growth in employees. These will have to work unsupervised and in a variety of roles which the founder does not fully understand.

You may have outstanding products and ample funds but if your staff dealing with manufacturing, logistics, selling, delivering, getting paid, are incompetent, don't care, or are plainly dishonest, you will surely fail. I have visited and advised many good-sized companies who had such problems and the MD/founder was aware of these facts. Those that failed to deal with the problem ALL failed eventually.

Without able, motivated, honest staff who work hard and care about the company's performance there is no possibility of continuous growth and profits. You need all the other elements of a successful business, but without the right people it will be a short term or struggling enterprise.

2. HOW TO RECRUIT, TRAIN, MOTIVATE, AND REWARD NEW STAFF

Please note that this section is primarily aimed at adding new staff. Most of the comments are relevant to existing staff but they have somewhat differing needs. Importantly, they have experience of the actual company and which is not always what the senior managers or directors believe is the case.

If you are growing you will need a constant supply of new staff. If you are a larger company there will be a certain degree of staff turnover at all times for a variety of reasons. This sometimes allows a company to refresh itself with new ideas. I maintain that all companies, large or small, should recruit the best people they can afford. Trying to cut costs on remuneration does not lead to a hardworking, motivated, achievement-led team. It is better to have one well-paid, high-quality individual than two of lesser capability.

3. RECRUITING ISSUES

Recruiting is without doubt an area of considerable personal opinion as to methodology and language used. Over the recent past the use of the internet has transformed wide areas of recruitment practice. As a result I will give here my personal beliefs which have worked successfully for me over many years. However, it is important for you that you develop your own methods.

Personally I have not liked to use recruitment agencies, who are expensive and can tend to keep on file details of staff they have recruited for you. They then sometimes call up those people with new job offers and cause quite some dissatisfaction. Certainly when I finally used executive recruiters at the insistence of our non-exec directors it turned into an unpleasant, expensive and destructive episode.

4. HOW TO RECRUIT

The first step in recruiting new staff is to write down very clearly what the job is supposed to be, its duties and responsibilities clearly understood. A full job description must be developed together with some indication of career progression opportunities. This should define who will be in charge of the new person (who they report to) and who, if any, what staff will report to them.

There are a large number of websites offering job description templates but many of these seem to be quite lengthy which I believe can be wrong. An attempt to write a job description so that all actions and possible outcomes are covered can end up being confusing and counter-productive. Such descriptions can lead to an employee using it to avoid doing something which is not properly described but within the meaning of the job description. Alternatively, it can lead poor managers to harass a disliked subordinate.

A good job description should at the minimum (as discussed above) outline the main management structure and the purpose of the post. In defining the purpose of the post and having a good set of corporate objectives most outcomes should be covered.

By recruiting the best people you can afford and giving them maximum freedom to carry out their duties, the problems of managing a company will be much reduced. Too often a job description is nothing more than a list of instructions on how to carry out a range of jobs to be done with little freedom for initiative.

My advice is, choose good people; describe the

starting point and the outcomes expected then let them get on with it. If they do not succeed replace them as soon as possible.

It will be vital that you have a well-defined and understood management structure for your company. This is discussed more fully in a later section. This may seem to be somewhat over the top for junior posts but in fact will often pay off in employee engagement. They will feel needed, informed, valued, and consequently feel good about joining the company.

The next task is to define the characteristics you want in the new recruit. For example, what are the levels of education and qualifications needed as a minimum, and what will be desirable beyond these minimums. I eventually fully embraced doing Personality Profiling and Aptitude Testing for virtually everyone in the company, especially at the more senior levels. I also found the BELBIN team role evaluation exceptionally valuable. We found that sharing these evaluations with others in our team helped the team to function more effectively as the members got to understand each other's motivations more fully.

There are a wide range of personality/aptitude tests available, some free, some charged for. I hold that it is well worth paying for these tests as they tend to be more tested and better thought out. I recommend the Thomas International range of personality profiling and the BELBIN tests for team role advice. There are books published by BELBIN which are well worth the read.

For my part I was usually regarded as competitive and aggressive, which in many ways is true, but this was mainly aimed at taking the team forward. I have always been a team player but tended to want to be the team leader. In Thomas International PPA tests I was shown to have high levels of both Dominance and Influencing, with corresponding low levels of Steadiness and very low levels of Compliance.

I wanted to be in charge and could easily explain why. On the other hand I was restless and needed change combined with a disregard for rules if they didn't seem appropriate. I didn't like too much detail unless a result depended on it, in which case I could be very picky indeed.

Despite all this, I really liked being in a team and performed best when in such an arrangement. I totally recommend treating the employees of a company as members of a team and recruiting with that in mind. Of course there will be many teams in a large company, but they should all feel that that they are part of the total team. It is the directors and managers who must create this feeling. For my part working for Hewlett Packard instrumentation was the closest I came as an employee to enjoying this arrangement. The whole company was comprised of small teams but we all felt engaged in the overall team and competed to make the biggest contribution.

I BELIEVE MOST STRONGLY THAT TREATING ALL STAFF AS MEMBERS OF A TEAM IS FUNDAMENTAL TO SUCCESSFUL GROWTH.

I used this idea in Densitron and it worked well for a long time until I handed over the CEO role. The company became progressively run more by command and control methods. I think the result is best illustrated by the fact that the company is now valued at around one third of its value at flotation in 1986. Hopefully it will recover in the future.

5. HOW TO TRAIN STAFF

Training should be seen as a continuing process. Part will be *skills specific to the job*, other parts more to do with *company and personal development*. For my part I chose to keep attending advanced training at colleges and or business schools throughout my career.

Sometime after becoming the Chairman of a public company I attended a well-regarded business school to learn more about being a Chairman. Fundamentally, at that stage I didn't really know the difference from being an MD. To my surprise no-one on the course or even the lecturer had been a Chairman and I ended up in the role of assistant lecturer, all at the cost of several thousand pounds.

I developed a good way to encourage training at Densitron. We issued a red briefcase to all employees, in which were kept their personal records of appraisals and progress in the company as the years passed by. Appraisal was on a regular basis and at the minimum was once a year. Individuals were put in charge of their own training. At appraisal, future training needs were discussed, agreed, and noted in the briefcase. Staff then had to seek out for themselves where to get this training. The company paid for the training and a full record of the results was examined at the next relevant appraisal. If the individual had not carried out the agreed training there was no possibility of a pay rise. If the results were poor then the pay rise would be restricted and promotion not likely.

Continuous training is a vital part of a vibrant progressive company. It is interesting that it is endemic in teaching and the armed services. It is not so prevalent in the smaller private companies and maybe explains part of the reasons many do not grow and progress.

6. MOTIVATION

Having recruited high quality staff and trained them well, there remains the task of keeping them motivated. Of course almost by definition such staff will tend to be highly motivated individuals. However, there is a very strong case for the directors and managers to pay attention to overall motivation and ensure that few, if any, staff are not performing to the best of their abilities.

This is not something that can be done by a stirring speech made by the Chairman or other senior managers at special events. It must be an almost daily drip feed of good news or other information.

7. IF YOU 'SPIN', EMPLOYEES WILL KNOW

What to me has loomed large in listening and

reading about motivating, is this subject of '**Spin**' and it seems to me that there is a case for discussing the use of language in business which arises from this concept of **'Spin'**. In communicating with the staff of a company either in writing or by discussion, the nature of the words and the way they are used is paramount. Many senior managers are self-deluding about their ability to inform and inspire their staff. I believe that a lot of the time they underestimate the innate intelligence and common sense of most people. It has always struck me how many times the so-called 'workers' on the shop floor are more aware of the difficulties in the firm than the senior management. The current run of programmes on television dealing with experts trying to help family and other companies is clearly indicative of it. It is rather sad how many of these people who have built up quite a reasonably successful business or inherited a family business are totally incapable of seeing the wood from the trees.

Returning to this word, **'Spin'**, because I think it is where the self-delusion starts to come in. In the past, before the word 'spin' was used existed a much better word, 'dissembling'. This was where a set of words were put out with the principle intention of hiding the facts. A good example is, of course, where somebody is sacked from a senior position or in either politics or in a business, and the canard is put out that they are returning to their family to spend more time with their children or they want to pursue other interests. Everybody is aware of what has happened but none the more for that it is felt better to dress up the truth with these weasel words.

The insidiousness in doing this, is that as the ordinary staff and workers of a company perceive more and more of this 'spin' or 'dissembling', the more it is seen as lying, and the more they perceive lying, the less they believe in their senior managers and the trust in their work. This can get to such proportions that almost nothing that senior management says is taken at face value. Everybody starts to interpret what the words are, what they mean, and what should have been said instead. Rumour abounds, and as a consequence attempts to efficiently manage the firm are lost.

I believe 'spin' and 'dissembling' have derived from a close association with the necessary process in selling, which tries to highlight the best features of a product or service. In fact they are materially different. Whereas good selling means highlighting the genuine benefits that a product brings to the purchaser, 'spin' and 'dissembling' are an attempt to hide the facts for long enough for some other purpose to be pursued. Therefore, for senior managers in a company to truly communicate with their staff, I think it is important that they understand the difference between 'spin', 'dissembling', and 'lying', or others such as 'deception', 'exaggeration', or 'misinformation'.

I give as an example the happenings of my old firm. They have changed their stated product policy on several occasions, which has not led to clarity of purpose. The company certainly hasn't gone onto success. However, the people who most matter are the people within the company and it would be interesting to know whether they still really believe the words that are put in front of them. I doubt it.

What I believe to be true about Densitron, I believe to be true about a range of other companies. I suspect that Marks and Spencer and Sainsbury's, amongst the larger companies, have also suffered a disconnection from belief by the staff working for them.

There seems to be a reliance on mechanistic approaches rather than understanding what the business is, where it should be going; how profits should be made and then communicating clearly to all of the staff, thus engaging them in the process to everybody's benefit.

The various senior management gurus who have been recruited to these well-publicised companies have come out with the same sort of mantra as I was highlighting for Densitron. They talk about Mission Statements, realigning the company, downsizing various elements, increasing the efficiency, improving the supply chain etc., until ultimately nobody really believes in anything and management turn to 'spin' to hide from the facts, and to persuade people that everything is all right. But once 'spin' is disbelieved it is self-defeating. The more you spin, the more it is understood to be spun, the less everybody believes anything you say.

What then am I advocating for the senior managers within companies?

I believe that you should go as close to the truth as it is possible to do when talking to the staff, subject only to commercially sensitive areas where disclosure could damage the business. However even in those areas I think you could indicate clearly that you know what you are doing. Most people will understand that. However, in being able to communicate you must have some sort of mastery over language and I think that management time spent learning how to use language and to speak properly is time well spent. It has to be a capability that is built by experience, by talking in small meetings, then larger meetings and if at all possible, publicly. There is never any harm in saying that you do not know, or do not understand, as long as you say so and mean it. The crime is to spin an answer.

Clear, honest statements of intent in plain language without the obfuscation are to everybody's merit.

8. DIRECT REGULAR CONTACT BETWEEN MANAGERS AND STAFF

The most potent motivator for all staff is regular contact with the most senior staff who know how the company is doing, and where possible, can interact with individuals at all levels. The ability for the MD to talk to everyone and be knowledgeable about individuals' roles is a very powerful motivator.

Over the last few years there has been a series of TV programmes about MDs of large companies going into their own companies under cover of being a new trainee to see how it has been working. Almost without exception they had lost touch with their own companies and were shocked at the poor practice that became uncovered by this simple ruse. To their credit they moved to change this situation BUT why had it occurred in the first place?

Basically it is laziness and the mistaken belief that any company can be run by someone who 'understands the numbers'. I say, "OH NO THEY CAN'T." The top people must understand the business in detail and interact with the staff on a regular basis. Obviously in very large companies this becomes difficult, but I feel that in those cases the MD must have a team around him who can take care of this important action.

At another level, getting the company referred to in the press, winning awards, appearing on TV will pay off, and making announcements about the company or its staff achieving some outstanding work locally or for charity will build pride. Pride will lead to motivation which in turn will create better, more reliable products, and not least, great customer service.

It is just as vital that the top people do this personal contact work as well as understanding the numbers.

3. SEVEN CORPORATE OBJECTIVES

I created a list of **7 Corporate Objectives** that were fundamental to the company. These were printed in booklet form and given to all applicants whilst being interviewed and discussed fairly fully to ensure that they were compatible with our overall objectives. This practice was started whilst we were a start-up company and remained central to our management throughout my stewardship.

The idea of these **Objectives** is to provide a simple framework on which daily decisions can be taken.

By writing down, in order of importance, the main reasons for the company to be in business, each employee is supplied with a simple checklist for decision making. If a difficult decision is to be made then it should be checked against these Objectives one by one. It if fails against any of the first two, it should be rejected. The best decision will meet all of these main Objectives.

To a large extent the first Objective of Continuity covers all of the following Objectives. The company cannot be continuous if it fails on the other Objectives.

1. CONTINUITY

Everybody, customers, suppliers, employees, bankers etc., need the company to remain in continuous business. No decision should ever be taken which threatens the future effective operation of the company. For example, we should not spend too much money, cheat the tax requirements, make losses, employ criminals or lazy people. We should not take orders larger than we have money to finance. We must have enough new products and train ourselves for the future and be enthusiastic.

CONTINUITY is the number one priority.

2. PROFIT

Profit is the reward we get for a well-run company. It rewards the employees by better pay and working conditions. It rewards the investors with dividends to encourage them to keep investing. It rewards the suppliers with bigger business, and it rewards customers with better products. However, more importantly, it provides the increased money for the company to grow into the future with the premises and people to run it properly.

3. CUSTOMERS

Everybody understands that we need customers, but how do we get them and keep them? Firstly, we should look at customers as somebody who needs to buy things to run their business. If we offer them products which are superior to the competition they will want to buy from us. So therefore, the main way to get customers is to offer them superlative and new products. To keep them we must back that product up with top grade service: salespeople who know the product and customer engineers who can answer the questions; a delivery service which gets the goods there in time, and a financial service which ensures the end result is timely and profitable. We must be seen by customers as an enthusiastic, caring, efficient supplier of modern competitive products.

4. GROWTH

For many reasons companies need to grow, but it is often difficult to decide by how much and then to actually achieve that growth. The most important reason to grow is that it is safer than not growing.

It is regarded that growth of Balance Sheet assets is the fundamental underpinning of all other forms of growth. Whilst obviously sales revenues and reported profits are important, it is the net asset situation on the Balance Sheet which is the specific determinate of growth. The security of the Balance Sheet should not be jeopardised in order to manipulate reported profits.

By growing we can increase salaries, recruit new people with new ideas, encourage investors to continuously invest, and help our customers grow. We should aim to grow at being 'better than the rest' of our industry, then we can be safe against decline or failure.

5. OUR PEOPLE

Basically, a company is only a theoretical concept. In reality it is a group of people working together for mutual benefit. Our policy is to encourage the most talented people to join the company at all levels. We then wish to tell them clearly what the company is trying to achieve and then let them work within these guidelines to fulfil their own ambitions.

The Board of Directors have issued this set of Objectives and then also a range of strategies and policies to help people meet the Objectives. Each year, each company or division writes down a forecast of achievable performance for the following year, and after agreement with the Board they set out to achieve this. In this way the people of the company help the company grow and secure for themselves a growing and satisfying career.

In the circumstances of the modern global economies, it is important that everybody accepts the need for continuous training to update and improve the skills within every individual. Such training is a joint responsibility and whilst the company should expect to lead in the matter, it is also required that every individual ensures that their training fits them for their role within the company.

6. MANAGEMENT

The management of a company is the method by which it organises its people to carry out its Objectives. It is obviously necessary that everyone in the company goes in the same direction so that maximum results may be achieved. The directors of the company decide what the company is trying to achieve, and then appoint various managers to carry out the agreed policies.

In my work I have given as much responsibility as possible to each individual by a system of setting objectives to achieve at all levels.

(Management by Objectives)

It is not expected that every action is controlled by a central, powerful group issuing orders. My method is to encourage everyone to understand the overall company objectives set out in this document and then arrange their own actions to follow the same path.

7. CITIZENSHIP

OBJECTIVE:

To honour our obligations to society by being an economic, intellectual and social asset to each nation and each community in which we operate. All of us should strive to improve the environment in which we live. As a corporation operating in many different communities throughout the world, we must make sure that each of these communities is better for our presence. This means identifying our interests with those of the community; it means understanding the uniqueness and qualities of other societies and ensuring that through our contacts with them we improve mutual understanding. The wider our trade and the more inter-dependence and understanding we achieve the more likely we are to achieve our own ambitions.

Wherever possible we should seek to make a contribution to whatever society we find ourselves working or living in. If we respect other people and their societies they will be more likely to respect ours. In turn our own self-respect will grow.

4. THE IMPORTANCE OF STRUCTURE

1. SOME IDEAS

Company structure is a very complex subject and there are a wide variety of types. This is even more the case when internet-based structures are included. However, a management structure is intended to allow management to take place and inform staff on matters of authority, responsibility, reporting, and control. To this end most structures will in the final analysis be based upon human values and consequently have much in common with each other.

> **The competitive, administrative formation verses the creative, innovative corporate structure.**

2. TWO MAIN STRUCTURES AND THEIR CHARACTERISTICS

I believe there will always be the inherent danger that a

company based solely upon 'competent administration' has in-built deterioration within the structure. If there are no self-regenerating creative initiatives, all products and services will ultimately be challenged by competing ones and start to go into decline.

What then can be done for those companies who wish to be well run but also have availability of vibrant new products and a future?

3. BUSINESS PLANS

Firstly, it has to be accepted that there is no way that the 'competent administrator' will be able to evaluate projects put forward to him or her by creative, innovative individuals. Within most companies that base their fundamental management on competent administration, there is some form of review body that looks at new products and projects. This body, whatever it is called, requires a 'business plan'. This must be written in such a way that it shows the precise amount of money to be spent on Research and Development; how much on creating prototypes and production; how much revenue will be attributed to a product's lifecycle, gross margins and return on investment over a five-year period. Many, many fruitless hours are spent in companies creating such business plans. Nearly all are utter balderdash.

There is no way that a creative, innovative person can establish such a structure without total guesswork.

However, against time they learn the rules of the game and realise that if they do not produce a

'Business Plan' which meets the company's requirements, their projects will not go forward. They learn the criteria and they generate business plans that meet all the criteria; these are endorsed without much questioning and go forward. Sometime later, the review body meets again to find their project is not meeting the business plan and either chop it in half or continue to pour money into it, still on a guesswork basis.

4. PEOPLE VERSUS STRUCTURE

All of this chaos derives from the fundamental assumption that the world is a predictable, manageable place. 'Competent administrators' believe in structures, reporting lines and detailed, accurate reports. They sit and analyse the data coming to them against defined criteria over time as to what is successful and unsuccessful. They require that the whole structure provide them with the information on which they can make judgement.

People are purely incidental items who get pushed into this structure according to set criteria determined by HR. In general, the managers are not made responsible for the people they recruit. People are identified by numbers and they either succeed or fail according to the set criteria whilst the company proceeds on its mechanistic progress.

Okay, let's go forward to potential solutions.

If it is the case that the 'competent administrator' can never understand the creative innovator and this must necessarily lead the company into a rigid hierarchical structure, then it must be true that the company should be headed in some form or the other by a creative, innovative individual. The difficulty is that an enormous number of creative, innovative individuals do not like and cannot carry out competent administration, the lifeblood that is vital for any larger enterprise.

5. RESPECT FOR OTHERS

The first requirement is that creative innovative individuals, particularly designers, should be trained in certain elements of competent administration. They should understand and respect the fundamentals of accountancy.

Accountancy can sometimes be treated with too much respect. It is really simple addition and subtraction overlaid with layer upon layer of opinion rules. All that is really necessary is to spend a period of time understanding these rules. The addition and subtraction is relatively simple. It is the opinions/rules that overlay it that are important and I suggest that all creative, innovative individuals should have an intensive course on the assumptions that underlay the accountancy profession.

The beginnings of my structure now begin to emerge.

6. SYSTEM

An individual who is creative and innovative but who understands the elements of competent administration is the right person to grow a company. That person should work in very close connection with a colleague who is a competent administrator. The competent administrator should be seeking to create a regularised structure and reporting system, but it should be subservient to the creative, innovative pulse.

The central difference between the CI (Corporate Innovative) company compared to a CA (Corporate Administrator) company is in the treatment of people. In a CI company, people are central. The first process is to ensure that the best quality people with the best brains and attitude are always recruited and that the structure of the company is built around them, rather than having to confirm to a pre-existing formation.

As an example, if you have an extremely talented inventive engineer but there is nobody in the structure to whom they can report, create a new configuration that suits the way they want to work rather than impose a system that they have to follow.

This type of process was carried out very successfully at Bletchley Park in the code-breaking exercises. The whole of that magnificent achievement was based upon the talents of individuals and not upon a management structure, although there was one. In many areas it was chaotic, but it was always innovative and problem solving.

7. LEADERSHIP

So, therefore, a CI company must be led by a creative, innovative individual and that person should ensure that the recruitment policies throughout the company stress the importance of the qualities of the people. If necessary there could be some form of Personnel or Human Resource management, but the recruitment and remuneration of people in the company should not be delegated to this third party organisation. They can research solutions, suggest ideas, develop criteria, oversee and help, but not actually do the recruitment and management of people.

8. MANAGERS' RESPONSIBILITY FOR THEIR OWN STAFF

Managers should be made to recruit their own people and to remunerate them on the basis of their position and performance. There should not be a rigid pay structure. The company should be prepared to pay for the individual performance in each of the areas. (A common pay scale across a wide range of people is currently what is killing some organisations. Staff in London are unable to live on the salaries that are quite viable in Newcastle. Perceptive management would recognise these differences.)

It is, therefore, vital that a modern-thinking, creative company should have a very positive people policy, articulated and implemented at Board level. Management should concern itself with the management of people rather than the consequences of the people's actions. The success of the company will grow out of the capabilities of its employees, not upon edicts issued from on high about required achievements.

The competent administrators will ensure that the facts and figures being collated are accurate and meaningful, but the judgement on them will be carried out by the creative individual.

9. TRUST AND LEADERSHIP

What this structure demands is that a large measure of trust and responsibility is given right the way down through the company. Don't expect creative, innovative individuals to justify every penny they spend. A funding allocation should be made based upon their competence, then they should be allowed to spend their budget and pursue their ideas with vigour and with a flexible central authorisation. This, of course, will send shivers down the spine of every competent administrator!

I would, however, close with some wise words of a past colleague of mine who once said: *"How can you expect people to manage other people? Most people cannot manage their own lives. They therefore should not think in terms of managing others, but becoming leaders."*

What is required for a creative company, is leadership. The leaders should want to be respected and trusted and, in order to gain that fine position, they should respect and trust others. They should not rely upon rigid reporting and dry statistics.

Understand people for what they are, have faith in them, and only employ those you respect and trust. Then reward them with a sensible pay scale, plus an occasional 'thank you', both monetary and verbal.

A company must be turned into a human workplace where ideas and creativity are welcomed, not a grinding machine based upon hierarchy and structure.

This type of company requires that managers (leaders) have to be excellent at understanding and encouraging people. It is very hard work particularly on the emotions, but it is most rewarding not least to the company itself.

10. COMPANY REPORTING STRUCTURES

All working environments have some form of organisational structure through which they gather information, make decisions, and communicate those decisions as needed to those working in the enterprise.

There are a very large range of structures that are used throughout the working environment and even those that are perceived to be similar can be made totally different by the individuals working within them. It can be very important to understand the organisation's structure before you join it.

For example, the Armed Forces have a very well-defined organisational structure and it is crucial to your progress or peace of mind that you understand it very well indeed. Other enterprises such as software development companies will have a less rigid structure and be more flexible to people working within it. It will often be the case when you first start work that a company will not be prepared to discuss organisational matters at interview, but it does not do any harm to ask. As your career progresses it gets more and more important to understand an organisation's structure.

Two major distinctions are structures that are diversified and collaborative compared to those that are tightly held in a hierarchy with strong chains of command.

Within the three sectors, PRIVATE COMPANIES use pretty well all forms of structure whilst the PUBLIC SECTOR tends to have a more hierarchical and rule driven structure. The VOLUNTARY SECTOR probably has the most diversified and collaborative approach.

Your personality and engagement profiles will help you to understand how well you are likely to react to these varied approaches.

11. THE HIERARCHICAL TOP-DOWN PYRAMID STYLE MANAGEMENT STRUCTURE

The *hierarchical top-down pyramid style management structure* is by far the widest used throughout the world. As an enterprise grows it needs to ensure that more and more information flows upwards very easily and decisions are delivered quickly and accurately downwards.

Example:

Using the *Armed Services* as an example, the smallest unit is often 5 people who have a low-ranking NCO in charge of them. This is because a greater number than 5 can be too complicated to manoeuvre in stressed or critical situations. However, a unit of 5 cannot be deployed in a strategic way so there will be formed a group of 5x5 controlled by a higher level of NCO. This logic is maintained all the way to the top so that the whole Army can respond very rapidly to orders issued by the officer in charge at the top. Maybe this is a field marshal, or for smaller campaigns a brigadier, etc. Once understood, this structure can be changed very flexibly depending on circumstances. Our military structures could be a useful field of study, as most other structures are more or less easily derived from them. All military forces tend to follow this arrangement.

12. UNDERSTANDING AND GROWING PRIVATE COMPANIES AND EMPLOYMENT

Private companies are mostly started by a single individual or a small group of collaborators. They will understand what they need to do and communicate directly with each other, often without a clear structure of management. As an enterprise grows it will take on extra specialised staff such as design engineers, bookkeepers, salesmen, machine operators, etc. By this stage the original team will have identified specific roles for themselves and will have these new staff join their specialism.

A growing company should create a Board of Directors to direct and control the activities of the company.

At the top will be a Chairman of the Board who will act as a focus for all activities and supervise the meetings of the Board.

The Chief Executive (Managing Director) will be given the task of running the company on a day-to-day basis and he will have, reporting to him, a range of specialist directors. For example, Finance Director, Production Director, Sales Director, Human Resources Director, Technical Director. There can be more but more than 6 is undesirable. Under each director will be a hierarchy of people arranged in management structure based upon the one given above for the armed services.

If you will join a company at some level within such a structure, it is vital that you quickly determine who you report to and who reports to you. Employees need to identify the rules and ethos under which the company works. The earlier this is done the better. If possible, get to understand as much about this before you join. Company websites may give you valuable insight and will repay study if you show at interview that you have studied these features. Even if you are joining at a very junior level bosses will be flattered that you have shown such initiative. For more senior posts it is vital to have this information. Do not expect to become employed if you have not learnt something about the company who is interviewing you. It costs a lot of time and money to carry out a range of interviews and you should respect this investment.

Many companies these days are part of a group encompassing several other companies, often with different names. In your career progression you may move between different parts of the same company or alternatively move to different but related companies.

All registered companies are owned by shareholders and it is the job of the directors to run the company to their benefit. If it is a private family company then it is likely that the shareholders will be family members and still working in the company.

Larger companies may well be public companies listed on a Stock Exchange. These may still include the founders as shareholders but there are strict rules about how these companies are managed, and the external shareholders must be cared for and kept up-to-date. Outside shareholders will be investing in the shares for two types of return benefit. One is an increase in the value of the shares so that a profit can be made if they increase in value. The other is by the company paying a dividend to the shareholders based upon the profits of the company.

Of course if the company does not make profits and the shares fall in value then the shareholders will lose money. Investing in shares is a source of capital to grow the firm but if anything goes wrong they lose the most as they get paid out last, after employees, the tax man, and banks.

See Addendum 1 for an example of Financial Reporting in a real Public Company.

5. THE THREE MAIN WORK PLACES

1. UNDERSTANDING YOUR CUSTOMERS' STRUCTURE TO INCREASE SALES

The numbers and statistics given in this article have been derived from a variety of sources. They are not intended to be precise but are accurate enough for the purposes of describing the nature and structure of the UK jobs market.

There are approximately 30 million people in employment in the UK, with 2.6 million unemployed.

There are effectively three main types of employers, which are:

1. **THE PRIVATE SECTOR** – which accounts for around 73% of the employed workforce;

2. **THE PUBLIC SECTOR** – which accounts for around 25% of the employed workforce;

3. **THE CHARITABLE / VOLUNTARY SECTOR** – which accounts for around 2% of the employed workforce.

Detailed examples of these are given later in this paper but there is a direct connection to 'job sectors' in our links section to a very informative part of our website.

Each of these sectors have somewhat differing employment characteristics and reward systems which are important to understand when trying to decide on a career path. Again what follows comprises broad generalities but more specific information is available elsewhere on the site.

2. THE PRIVATE SECTOR

The private sector can be seen to be the largest employer, being some 3 times larger than the next largest, the public sector. The private sector is essentially the practice of capitalism. It is where the bulk of new wealth is created and its taxes and donations effectively fund the rest of the economy. Several other economic models have been tried over centuries but capitalism has delivered, in combination with democracy, the biggest increase in wealth and health when compared to other systems of economic activity. This sector organises itself through the creation of a range of different types of companies. They are all aimed at using capital within a defined business structure to create new wealth which in turn pays for income/taxes and reinvestment. Some need small amounts of capital where others, such as oil or aviation companies, need extremely large sums of working capital.

Examples of such organisations are:

1. The *Sole Trader* which comprises an individual working for himself and maybe employing a small number of other people.

2. A *Partnership* where a group of individuals come together as partners, sharing the rewards and the investment dangers on an agreed basis. The partners' personal assets are used to underpin this activity and are at risk at all times.

3. A *Limited Liability Partnership* (LLP). This is similar to an actual partnership but the partners have put limits on the extent of their liabilities.

4. A *Limited Liability Company* (Ltd). The formation of a company allows the ability to create shares indicating part ownership of the company. Such shareholders need not work in the company but by purchasing shares they invest capital in the company. Their capital investment is at risk but their exposure to loss is limited to this investment and not any other wealth they may have. Hence *Limited Liability Company*. This structure has been responsible for the vast bulk of wealth creation and was an English invention to help fund international trade by ships. Shareholdings can be very different between individuals and there are rules to deal with disputes, etc.

5. A *company limited by guarantee*. Which is where the shareholding is the same for all shareholders and the extent of their liability is normally very low. Many sports/golf clubs are organised in this way.

6. A *Public Company (PLC)*. This is a Limited Company that has arranged for all or part of their

shares to be openly traded on the Stock Exchange. This is for larger companies in general but there are a range of Stock Exchanges which deal with a variety of sizes and types of company. Once a company has issued its shares onto a Stock Market they have to follow strict rules of behaviour and are subject to votes by the shareholders, the majority of whom will not be employed by the company. Public Companies are a prime source of investment for pension funds and savings.

The management and career structure for each of these companies are discussed later. Around 19% of employees in private companies are graduates, which totals 4.4 million people and numerically the largest number of graduates in employment. Selling to them requires the use of highly diverse methods.

3. THE PUBLIC SECTOR

The public sector includes all people engaged in carrying out work for government ministries, departments, or local authority organisations. They account for spending around 45% of all the money spent in the economy but only 25% of the employment. The money they spend is mainly raised from the private sector in the form of taxes such as: income tax from individuals, corporation tax from companies' profits, VAT, NI payments by individuals, council tax, inheritance tax, road tax, duty on drinks cigarettes and petrol, etc., etc. These taxes, when paid by public employees, are paid out of the money already paid out as taxes by private organisation, and so in a way are taxed twice.

At the government level the organisations are divided into ministries or departments, for example, Health, Defence, Home Office (Prisons and Police), Education, etc. A full list can be found on Wikipedia.

At the local authority level there a very wide range of expenditures and again these can be found on local government websites. The largest expenditure is usually on education.

Graduates form 37% of the public sector employees but this equates to 2.2million people or half the number employed in the private sector. It does however mean that being qualified is of major importance to a career in the public sector. One reason is of course the huge size of the educational and health sectors. Selling to this sector involves responding to formal enquiries and competing mostly on price.

4. THE CHARITABLE/VOLUNTARY SECTOR

This sector is by far the smallest of the three main sectors, with only 2% of the working population, but it has the highest percentage, 38%, of graduate members.

Despite its small size it does have a very large number of organisations within it, ranging from large charities such as Oxfam through to very small local initiatives involving very few people.

The above numbers are for those who are

employed by relevant registered organisations, but of course there are a very large number of people who give their time for free. Selling to charities is a combination of the private and public sector.

Over the recent past the development of the internet and resulting growth of mobile hardware such as iPhones, iPads, and laptop computers with WiFi, has created a much more flexible and variable way of working. This has led to Hot-Desking, working from home or from independent offices. Personally I still believe it vital that humans are able to have regular face-to-face contact and meetings for effective working processes. In this way an understanding and explanation of corporate structure is important for employees. This can only happen if the owners and managers of businesses have thought about these matters in some detail and explained the issues to all the staff in a way they can understand.

Whatever structure is approached it should be to ensure that fundamental business activities are clearly identified. Further, there are sufficient chains to provide clear reporting, giving both financial and activity based information. All directors are jointly and severally liable for the company and must be able to access all relevant information. It is their duty to ensure that the company is acting lawfully in the interests of the shareholders. A great deal of focus should be put on customers and customer satisfaction. Without sufficient satisfied customers any business will ultimately fail. Of particular importance is the process for dealing with complaints. Too often in Britain a complaining customer is seen as a nuisance, whereas properly handled good publicity can result.

6. THE PEOPLE WHO INFLUENCE A COMPANY'S PERFORMANCE

Shareholders, the Board, the managers, the employees, the customers, the suppliers, the governments and professional organisations.

If you choose to grow, all of the people listed above will in one way or the other impact on your company. It pays to be aware of their interests and powers.

1. SHAREHOLDERS/OWNERS

As we are talking about growth you will by this stage have determined which structure you have decided upon for your company. Whether it be a Sole Trader, a Partnership, or Registered Company there will be people somewhere who own it. Their needs and opinions will have to form a very significant part of your thinking. If you, with or without colleagues, are the owner/s that is very fortunate. However, the greatest number of people are working in someone else's company as a director, manager or general employee.

The first step in dealing with what can be a

complex situation is to understand your position in this structure and its decision making process.

In Ltd or PLC companies the shareholders have ownership in the company in proportion to the percentage of shares they hold. They can buy or sell shares as they like within the law. The powers they have are detailed in the Memorandum and Articles of Association. If you are a shareholder it is important that you understand these papers as they will determine what powers you have in influencing or controlling the company. If you are a shareholding employee it is even more important to understand your position.

EXAMPLES:

I had three very significant experiences concerning shareholding in a company. Two were in my own company; one when it was a Private Ltd Company and the other after it became floated on the London Stock Exchange as a public company. The third, which I discuss first, was as an employed manager/director in a privately owned company.

Broken Promises – Example:

The very first one was when I was headhunted into employment by a mid-sized private electronic company. The company was in some difficulty with falling orders and low profits. I was uncertain whether to take up their offer but they added the incentive that if I succeeded to recover the company I would be made a director and issued with a 10% shareholding. After two years I had brought in much new business and the company was growing profitably, so I asked for my rewards. Very naive at that time, and did not realise that although they called me Marketing Director, I was not legally registered as a director. I remained in ignorance of this fact and some months later I asked for my shareholding. They then told me that unfortunately the shares were by now too valuable to deliver this promise. I had been stupid enough to trust them and not have the offer in writing. This was a lesson that I did not always remember, sometimes to my cost.

The next occasion was after some years in my start-up company known as Taylor Miller Ltd, 'TM', which was a holding company that eventually became the floated company Densitron International PLC.

Shareholder Dispute – Example:

I had two initial investor directors who were the Managing Director and Finance Director of Hewlett Packard. At one stage when TM was doing very well with three subsidiaries (two manufacturers) the MD decided he wanted to leave HP and join TM. This he did at a salary far above what I was taking. Some time later he expressed dismay at how hard he was having to work and wanted to get out. To do this he needed to settle with me the largest shareholder. Consequently we had a shareholders and directors' meeting in a London hotel. I asked him what his proposal was to leave but he hadn't prepared any ideas at all. I had. I suggested there were 6 possible outcomes. I bought him out, he bought me out, we sold to another company and all left, we split the company in one of three ways.

I asked him if he could think of any other solutions and he agreed there were no other choices. I then said, "OK, choose one." His reply was that he didn't like any of them. This, from a man previously employed as the UK MD of Hewlett Packard.

As a result I made the final decision which was that I would buy him out and thus become a controlling shareholder with 61% (previously 31%). I had to borrow the money to do so but it turned out very well for me afterwards.

Ignorance – Example:

The final major experience was long after flotation and we had become a truly global company, and at one stage in the dot-com boom, a heavily backed share ultimately reaching a price of around £5 per share from a flotation value of 50p. I was visited by a major city merchant bank/stockbroker who asked me to use the opportunity to raise £50m for future use.

I declined (stupidly) because I had no project in mind to use such a large sum. I should have understood that such chances only come once and ultimately had to sell most of my shares at 8p. This happened because I had been ousted from the company through the machinations of a city financier who imagined he could make a fortune from some land we owned. He was wrong and the company has paid a very high price.

What is the lesson that I am trying to outline here? It is that companies will be owned by someone somewhere and they have legally defined real powers. It is vital that whether you are an employee or alternatively an owner, you understand the powers that the owners have. Pay attention to the legalities and if uncertain get professional advice.

2. THE BOARD OF DIRECTORS

Must be suitable to create growth

I am using the term 'director' here to also cover other structures such as partnerships, where there will be Managing Partners, etc. It is easy to check these structures on the internet. I am not so interested here in the legal issues but more the distribution of power. It may have been that when your company started there was little consideration given to these rules. However, as you are now considering significant growth full attention must be given to the roles and powers of the directors.

The controlling sequence is that the owners in one way or another own the company and there are legal powers and constraints placed upon them. They will, in the main, choose to create a Board of Directors to direct and run the company, although if not registered as a company but are, say, a partnership, the titles may be different.

Directors are charged with running the company to the benefit of the owners. It is for the owners to decide if their interests are being fully considered. Of course for most companies in their early growth stages the owners will probably also be the directors. However, if the owners are not actually the Board itself, it is up to them to check what is happening to the company and change the directors if necessary. The larger the company becomes, the more difficult it is to apply this controlling power. The most extreme example of this is that of the publicly traded companies on a Stock Exchange. Here the shareholders are often remote from the company and rely on the Annual General Meeting for the chance to act.

However, in this book I am trying to deal with the managed growth that occurs after a successful start-up has been achieved and the company is well financed and profitable. The growth factors in much larger companies are in more complex equations which I will deal with in a separate book.

Having dealt with the duties and liabilities of directors, we come to the task of actually creating and using a Board of Directors. How many shall we need? What will be their roles and titles, etc?

3. BOARD STRUCTURE

The standard structure has a CHAIRMAN whose initial role it is to organise, selecting and appointing the Board. Once a Board is created the Chairman will chair its meetings according to the wishes of the shareholders. The Chairman can be either non-executive (having no management role) or an executive chairman with relevant powers.

As an example of a Board of Directors there can be a Finance Director, a Sales Director, a Technical Director, a Human Resources Director, a Production Director, a Marketing Director and running the whole company – the very vital Managing Director. Finally, it is normal to have a company secretary who has no management role but will advise on legal matters if there is no Legal Director appointed.

As a company emerges from the excitement of a start-up it is usual to find setting up a Board of Directors somewhat difficult. It often happens that the role of director is merged/confused with the role of a manager. The difficulty with this situation is that Board meetings degenerate into management meetings dominated by whoever is the Managing Director. The discussions become very tactical and ignore the strategic issues. The Board meetings will become focussed on immediate problems and ignore the long-term view which is the vital responsibility of the directors.

4. THE ROLE OF THE DIRECTORS

The role of the directors is to understand the wishes of the shareholders and make plans for the more distant horizons. A five-year plan broken down into one-year Objectives would be one example of the Board's responsibility. The growth in the 'return on shareholders funds' is a fundamental consideration. Geographic presences will be another. Refining the Corporate Objectives and future product development within new markets should also be on the agenda.

5. GOOD AGENDAS HELP GROWTH

Whilst mentioning the agenda, it is worth stating that a vital part of the Chairman's role is to organise and publish to the Board a proper *agenda* for Board meetings. It has been my experience that for the vast majority of Boards (and also managers) agendas for meetings are far too long and complex. For a successful meeting the time allowed should be enough to allow full discussion without artificial constraints such as allocating specific timing to individual subjects. It is in my opinion that the agenda should allow proper time for each subject and hold the meeting in two sessions if necessary.

This is better than having unduly long meetings where people become bored and restless or not allowed to express their opinions. However, one cause of unduly long meetings is allowing members to continuously endorse and repeat what has already been said. A simple, "I agree with the Finance Director on this issue," is sufficient without repeating the whole substance again.

A well-constructed, informed, and active Board of Directors is vital to the healthy growth of a company. A Board need only meet from time to time; say, quarterly. Strategic issues do not (or should not) change quickly. It is confusing the roles of directors and managers that causes most of the problems.

6. SMALLER COMPANIES

Smaller companies, say up to £2m sales, do not need a large Board but less than 3 can cause difficulties as there may not be sufficient alternative opinions to allow an in-depth discussion. For example, for a smaller company a Managing Director, a Finance Director, and a Technical Director could be sufficient. The Technical Director could be substituted with a Sales Director of sufficient capability, or it is likely that the MD can carry out two or even three roles.

The two most ignored directorships in smaller companies are those of finance and technology. Most wrongly appointed is sales or marketing, which is often a confused mixture. It has surprised me how many quite large companies have an unsatisfactory Finance Director and often ignore the post entirely relying on the auditors to provide information and guidance. The main problem with Finance Directors is that they are frustrated Managing Directors. They long to run the company because they feel that they are the only one who 'understands the numbers'.

In starting, building, and running my company there became a long list of Finance Directors who manipulated the reports to guide the company in a direction they favoured. This included allocating overheads into the wrong departments, hiding improper development expenditure, and even on one occasion falsifying a VAT Return (identified in time to avoid trouble). On other occasions as a floated company the Finance Director lied directly to a stockbroker/analyst about a situation in Taiwan. I was left with the decision whether to contradict my Finance Director in public or leave the matter to be corrected later. I chose the latter but the damage had already been done. The real answer to this problem is for the other directors to become informed about financial matters. I found them very interesting and spent much time understanding our accounts, which allowed me to act as a brake on the most damaging occurrences.

My advice to you in growing your Board is to give a lot of thought. Go to courses at management colleges but above all find good, trustworthy people. Be totally intolerant of poor or deceptive performance. Ensure that your directors also attend regular training courses in their own and their colleagues' disciplines. Personally I have little faith in the short, punchy, evangelistic sessions offered by allegedly charismatic individuals. A proper short course (3-14 days) at an established management college will repay the investment many times over.

Being a director is an important and vital job, needing a lot of thought. It carries large penalties for wrong behaviour and deserves more thought than it is often given. A directorship is a long-term role which has in the UK, to our great disadvantage, tended to become a short-term tactical one. The dominance of the German and Japanese car manufacturers is solidly based on a long-term commitment. Our car manufacturing is now owned by foreign companies because of the short-term financial attitude of our investors combined with outdated technical capabilities and great salesmanship.

7. THE MANAGERS

As commented earlier the term '*manager*' could in many circumstances usefully be changed to '*leader*'. People may react negatively to the idea of being managed, with its direct link to the ideas of power, control, and manipulation. Being seen in many situations to be inadequate in knowledge about company processes, the term 'manager' has been largely demoted to almost a term of abuse. Inadequate managers tend to hide behind authority or control and do not command respect. Often this is due to over-promotion. A famous statement was, "People keep getting promoted until they reach their level of incompetence and there they remain." Thus, after a time a company will be managed by people all acting at their level of incompetence.

This can easily happen in family companies where the founding parent routinely appoints their children to positions for which they are not suited. Alternatively, they fail to bring in vitally needed outside expertise. Over 90% of the private family-style companies I have visited had this fault.

So let us discuss managers.

We have discussed the owners who provide the Investment and Working Capital. We have looked at the role of directors who are responsible to the shareholders for the efficient and successful use of the money. It is their role to create a viable strategic plan with clear objectives and time scales. Having done so, they appoint a group of managers to recruit, organise, and deploy a workforce capable of delivering the plans to reach the desired outcome or better. Thus the role of the management team is to bring the strategic plans to a successful conclusion.

Whilst the primary role of the directors is strategic, the managers are the tacticians. They will see things on a much shorter time scale than the directors. They will understand the longer-term strategies of the directors and be able to create action plans to deploy the assets, both human and inanimate, to maximum effect.

The directors will normally have several managers reporting to them but it is wise to limit this to 5 or less. A larger number of managers reporting to a single director will make them incapable of paying sufficient attention to what is happening. The company must have a management reporting system to enable them to monitor the work of the managers and change the plans if necessary.

A good management reporting system will be easy to read, accurate, but above all, timely. Many smaller companies rely on their auditors' annual report to determine whether they are successful and how profitable (or not) they are. Such annual reporting is far too slow for a growing company. For certain, cash flow matters can rapidly get out of hand during a period of fast growth. It pays to remember that you may be profitable but not generating enough cash to pay your bills. Either way, unprofitable or running out of cash, you will be either bankrupt or insolvent; neither a very good outcome.

Initially in Densitron we had monthly reporting for the key indicators, but ultimately our system became so sophisticated that it was largely real-time. We wrote our own software for a computer built by our Hungarian partners which in turn was an almost direct copy of a famous American brand. By today's standards it was very limited. All products were listed in the database, with who made them and what the costs were. As orders were placed, the computer noted what products were involved and what the in-store costs would be. It also knew when they were to be delivered and the price being charged. It therefore knew how much our gross profit would be and when we would receive it into our bank. It knew our overhead costs and therefore we could at any time not only know what our financial position was (GLOBALLY) but what it was likely to be in the following months.

As the orders were placed on us we knew immediately when they were due for delivery and thus had a forward forecast of our expected shipments, month by month into the future. This sort of thing is now routine for the more aware companies although I know many mid-sized outfits still do not have adequate reporting. In Densitron we had the basics in place in the 1980s.

Summarising 'managers', we can say their role is to ensure the efficient delivery of the outcomes detailed in the directors' strategic plans. They will be organised into a formal reporting structure that is understood by all staff and allows instructions to be issued with outcomes reported accurately and quickly.

The precise structure used to organise the managers will vary widely and there is no 'best' solution. The principles should be that it is easily understood by everyone and does not overload any manager by having too many staff reporting directly to them. A good minimum is 3 and a good maximum is 5. Anything over 8 will lead to serious problems. Anything under 3 will lead to conflict as it will leave one person telling another two how to do everything.

I recommend that some consideration is given to the idea of leadership. It is now probably impossible to dispense with the term 'manager' but if leadership values are considered when making an appointment, a better organisation may result.

8. THE EMPLOYEES

Your employees are the lifeblood of your company and I must repeat the guidance given earlier in the Corporate Objectives. You should always recruit the very best people you can afford and refresh them regularly by compassionately weeding out underperformers. It is a major part of the management team's responsibility to carry out the recruitment, training, deployment and monitoring of the employees entrusted to their management.

I found that the two most useful tools were those offered by Thomas International and Belbin.

Both of these systems and relevant books are available on the internet. It is better that you read and understand the original work rather than rely on an analysis by me.

By using these or other personality profiling systems you will achieve two very important things. Firstly, you will be more certain in your recruitment and the use of new staff, but more importantly you will enable your staff to understand themselves better and how they fit into balanced teams. I am a firm believer in using team structures at all levels within a company, at every level from the Board to the most junior post in the company.

Without any doubt people react better and more efficiently within teams that are well informed about their role in growing the company. I fear that two very important features of the British people are authority embedded in a bureaucracy. We were excellent in military matters and the administration of a Global Empire. Such management structures are not so applicable in today's working environment which has a much more open and flexible approach. The increasing use of technology to allow part-time and transient staff to operate effectively whilst located at differing geographic sites.

Whilst such flexible working methods are now an integral part of our working lives, I hold that for effective working, people must feel part of the organisation and get the chance to meet together on a fairly regular basis. Time spent in these meetings, if run effectively, will pay off in a more committed and effective work force. The top directors must be seen in and around about the company. They should make themselves available to listen to suggestions and discuss problems.

Elsewhere in this book I refer to Bill Hewlett and Dave Packard as my mentors in this approach. I have been asked by some people why I travelled so much during my building and running Densitron. The answer was that with such a huge diversity of products, people, and locations, something/someone had to ensure we were all travelling in the same direction.

Our main resource was talented sales and design engineers, not the products themselves. My successors made a huge mistake in deciding that the core competency was displays. In fact it was our engineering talent. Concentrating on displays resulted in a tremendous decline in the company and its capabilities. The Balance Sheet saw a decline of over £25m with the share value of the company becoming, at around £3.5m, a third of the 1986 flotation price.

The change resulted in most of the talent leaving to set up their own companies which now have cumulative sales and profits far in excess of the original parent. If ever there was an example of the importance of capable staff this must rank amongst the most dramatic.

I travelled worldwide to enable all of the people to see me and talk to me at least once annually. We arranged the Board meetings to take place at all the main locations of the UK, USA, Japan, and Taiwan. We also arranged training sessions for senior staff to coincide with the Board meetings, which spread the gospel even more widely.

I travelled over 5 million miles by air during this time (3.5 million with BA alone) – all very expensive but effective in growing the company.

9. THE CUSTOMERS

There is no doubt that your customers will have a huge role to play in the growth of your company. If they don't you are putting your company at great risk.

The type of goods that they buy, the price they pay, the quantity they order and for how long, will totally determine your future.

To repeat the Japanese mantra, 'The Customer is not the King, he is GOD', I do not personally hold such strong views but without exception customers should always be treated with great respect and courtesy.

Without much doubt the British approach to customers is severely lacking and sometimes even abusive. I cannot count the number of occasion when as a potential customer I was treated with disdain or even outright rudeness.

One particular occasions springs to mind from several years ago. I was looking to buy a new car and had been attracted to the Jaguar range. I went into our local Jaguar dealership and started looking at the various models on display.

I was left severely alone for some time but

eventually a salesman approached me and his first words were part of a longer interrogation. "Are you looking for a new or a second hand model, sir?"

I replied that I wasn't decided as I was just trying to understand what was on offer. Back he came. "How much do you want to spend? Will you need HP, sir?"

Price wasn't an issue, I truthfully replied. It was the comfort and performance that would finally decide.

"Do you have anything to trade?" came next. My reply was yes, but what I really wanted to do was understand the range, sit in possible choices, and then take a test drive.

"You will have to book for a test drive, sir. What are you driving at the moment?"

All of his questions were dripping with ill-disguised superiority. He plainly felt that I should have to prove myself worthy of being allowed near a Jaguar (today's Jaguar company is very different.)

At this point I walked out. At no time did he try to describe or pick up on my issues of comfort and performance. No wonder they went out of business.

There was an interesting follow-up to this episode because I wrote to the papers and my letter was published. As a result a variety of competitors contacted me and offered cars on loan for a week to carry an evaluation. This included SAAB, ROVER TRIUMPH, and others. I enjoyed several weeks of free high-quality motoring.

The strange thing was that after I had returned each of the cars nobody contacted me to sell me one of the models I had tested, but they let the press know what they had done. They were not really interested in securing a new customer. I bought a Rover because a friend who owned a garage said he would get one immediately (as opposed to the normal wait). He drove that day to Bristol from Greenwich to get it and brought it to my house. Customer service or what? I must say that the service offered these days by Amazon is exceptional.

Get to love and respect your customers or you will not prosper fully. On the other hand, you should expect them to pay a full price for this approach.

10. THE SUPPLIERS

Depending on the size and nature of your business the relationship with your suppliers will vary. In the early stages of your company you will be very dependent on the goodwill of your suppliers, whether it is for raw materials or finished goods. You will almost be in the role of supplicant begging for low prices, quick delivery, and credit.

As you grow, this relationship will gradually change. When you become a large or even dominant customer with a good credit performance you will be able to extract better and better terms from your suppliers. The extreme level of this situation is best illustrated by large Japanese companies, particularly in the car manufacturing business, but our supermarkets are not far behind. They will not only squeeze price but demand transparency on your costs and practices.

The Japanese even told steel manufacturers which mine to use. To be fair a lot of these actions were to improve quality. By eliminating any material or supplier whose performance proved unsatisfactory, the more standardised and reliable became their cars.

I remember in my early days in the consumer electronics industry, manufacturers had a person at the end of the production line with a rubber hammer. They switched the product (radio or TV) on and then listened to it whilst hitting it with the hammer. If it crackled or in any other way reacted to the hammer blows it was sent on to another line for remedial action. The Japanese pioneered the idea of eliminating faults before the product was finally tested. It is now common to see cars come to the end of the production line and start first time, to be driven away for delivery.

The selection of suppliers is of paramount importance to ambitious companies. Your relationship with them will determine your success in satisfying the needs of your customers.

During the building of Densitron I always visited suppliers regularly and walked along the production line. I would not buy from a supplier which could not demonstrate at every stage a commitment to quality. There were occasions when I initially refused to supply a customer with a product they asked me to source. I would visit the supplier and try to get my concerns addressed, after which I would agree to supply. If I couldn't do this I helped the customer move to a better supplier.

You owe it to your customer and your own company to deliver high-quality reliable products. This applies even to ultra-cheap products. A cheap car may not have the characteristics of an expensive one but it should be reliable and safe to drive.

7. PEOPLE MANAGEMENT

People management is a vital part of growing and demands continuous attention.

1. HOW TO MANAGE DIVERSE PEOPLE

As we are discussing growth it is a good time to consider the stage when the growing company operates in differing countries. This is a function that I found absolutely absorbing. Densitron operated in 22 different countries. There were obvious differences between our European operations and those in Asia, but there were also surprising differences in practice between European countries. Even more surprising were the language and commercial differences between the UK and the USA.

The English language that the Americans use is not the same as the UK. For example, I was once taken to task by one of the American directors for describing his suggestions as 'useful'. He explained that a waste paper basket was useful whereas his ideas were 'GREAT'. Apart from the unexpected language differences there were substantial commercial and legal practices that could trap the unwary. We had to fight a $2.5m court case on such a misunderstanding and were lucky to escape unscathed.

It is probably best to treat all overseas operations as individual cases rather than extensions of UK practice and law. This is not easy to remember at all times. In our CORPORATE OBJECTIVES listed earlier we stated that we aimed to be good citizens in every country we operated. We set out to obey the law and be a contributing asset in all locations. I believe that under my leadership we achieved that objective. It wasn't easy but was mostly achieved by having each of our subsidiaries managed by local people and allowing them to operate within our overall guidelines as interpreted by them for local operations.

We further enhanced this local management policy by offering the senior directors/managers a significant shareholding in the local enterprise. By being part owners they then had a strong personal interest in ensuring the company was properly run. They were allowed (in certain circumstances) to swap their local shareholding for main company shares, which as a floated company could be turned into cash. As always, a strong personal involvement leads to a strong motivation to have the company succeed rather than exploit the authority they had for personal gain.

On top of this policy of engagement was a practice of many and regular personal meetings between the whole management team. We held main Board meetings in all the main locations and held training meetings on a regular basis for virtually all the senior management. At these meetings the company's future plans were discussed and modified if needed. These meetings were somewhat expensive but were invaluable in guiding and motivating our managers. They in turn were expected to hold local meetings at which the company's plans and future products were discussed.

In addition to these regular planned meetings I personally travelled to all locations, especially Asia and the USA. As well as our own offices I visited all suppliers, meeting with their senior people to discuss the future. According to British Airways I travelled over 3.5 million miles with them and more was added flying with other airlines including JAL, United AA, Pan American, Continental, Alaskan, British Caledonian, Virgin, Cathay Pacific, Evergreen, Malev, Aeroflot, Quantas, Sunshine, Air France, Alitalia, SAS, Sabena, Catskill airlines, and some others I can't remember.

I visited every supplier we used and would not sell anything that seemed to me to be poorly made or lacking in some other way. Originally before we floated I visited as an ordinary individual and valued customer. In Japan however, I hit a problem after we floated in 1986 and I became a public company Chairman.

One of our most valued suppliers was Sanyo, where I was able to meet all the senior engineers and managers to discuss products and plan sales campaigns. The problem that arose was that as a Public Company Chairman I had suddenly acquired a higher status which demanded that I had to meet with Sanyo staff at the same level of hierarchy, i.e. Chairman!

This caused great upset, as if my status was not matched by Sanyo they would be seen as losing face. The problem that then arose was that the Sanyo Chairman nominated was from a subsidiary, and being in a comparatively huge company had no idea about our business or the products that interested us. Further to this, he spoke no English and I spoke very limited Japanese.

My main Japanese partner was unwell for the first meeting when this problem arose and I was accompanied by a relatively junior member of our staff who was hastily drafted in as an interpreter. This worked well for some time but at one stage I had to disagree with some suggestions made by the Sanyo Chairman and suddenly my junior interpreter became very embarrassed and ceased to translate.

At this point the meeting was abandoned and we returned to Tokyo, a 2hr plane journey. When we got back and our Japanese director questioned him, it turned out he had felt too junior to tell a Japanese Chairman that he was mistaken. It took some sophisticated thinking to overcome this problem but eventually we did so, but it caused an unfortunate delay in a major sales campaign.

2. TO GROW SAFELY THE SENIOR STAFF MUST REGULARLY MEET WITH PEOPLE THEY ARE RESPONSIBLE FOR

Returning to the importance of personal meetings, I hold that it is of paramount importance for senior people to visit and be seen to do so by as many of the staff as possible. It is also the case that such managers should know what is going on throughout the company.

The first time I met this approach was at Hewlett Packard in the early 60s when it was a scientific measuring instrumentation company still run by its two founders.

One day when visiting our Scottish factory at South Queensferry, I was having lunch in the canteen when Hewlett himself came and sat beside me with his lunch. We wore name badges at that time so he knew my name and I certainly knew him. He opened the conversation in a friendly manner and asked what position I held. I replied that I was a salesman covering part of South East England. He firstly said that HP salesmen were probably the most important people in the company. This was not necessarily true, but good to hear.

He then immediately asked me why the 681 sweep signal generator was not selling well in the UK. What a revelation, the most senior director and founder of the company knew that a single, not very expensive product was not selling well in one part of England. Luckily I knew the answer and he thanked me.

Based upon my experience in English companies I thought that would be the end of the matter. However, a few days later came a message from the USA factory making the 681, asking directly, "Who is Cliff Hardcastle?" They had been instructed to contact me and get the problem solved. At that moment I realised what a powerful tool knowing about your business in detail was.

3. AN EXAMPLE OF BAD PRACTICE

As Chief Engineer in a British company the MD

didn't even know I was in India running trials on new equipment and negotiating a £3m contract. He thought I was off ill. A very great difference in approach.

What does all the above add up to? It means that the senior people must be suitable for their post and that they in turn must get to know the company, its products, and most importantly people, in detail. They must ensure the products are fit for purpose. Most importantly they should reward, motivate, and value the staff by knowing who they are and what they do. Finally, let them know that you know them and care for their wellbeing.

4. HOW TO PRUNE INEFFECTIVE PEOPLE

Having dealt in some length with recruiting, motivating, and rewarding employees there arises the question about how to deal with non-performers.

People may have been wrongly selected or they could have been over-promoted. They might be suffering some personal stress or it may be that the company has changed. When a company grows strongly it often occurs that individuals cannot grow themselves as strongly.

This should become apparent at the regular appraisals but could occur unexpectedly. However, once the underperformance is identified it must be dealt with quickly, because their colleagues will have noticed and will resent non-performers dragging them back.

The first thing is to be totally honest with the individual. A private meeting with the appropriate manager should be arranged for the problem to be discussed in confidence and in depth. Where at all possible some form of remedial help should be offered. This might take the form of extra training or resources or redeployment in a more suitable post in the company.

Great effort should be put into this process and to a limited extent made known to their colleagues. It encourages staff to see colleagues being helped and supported in this way rather than just being sacked. These days there is considerable legislation surrounding employees and their welfare but in my opinion it is better that a company sets its own standards and doesn't hide behind legislation. Caring for your staff and providing appropriate training is always a sound investment.

Finally, however, there will always be some people for whom it is appropriate that they leave the company. A long time ago I read a book about management and it made the statement that in dealing with difficult staff matters you should be *ruthless in the decision but compassionate in the execution*. I found that to be very good advice indeed. Insisting on high standards is to the benefit of everyone involved in the company, from directors to part-time cleaners. Non-performers have to leave. However, they don't have to be destroyed in the process. Wherever possible we adopted an approach of trying to help them get a new job. This was not always possible but in trying we did demonstrate that we valued the person, it was only their skills that were not suitable. There are always cases which involve criminality or outright laziness. These should be dealt with less consideration but still with some compassion depending upon circumstances. They should always be dealt with honestly and not with a pretence of help.

Over the last few years I have been very flattered to have past employees that I have had to dismiss seek me out and thank me for the way they were dismissed, but with advice and honesty. In one case this had resulted in the individual self-appraising his arrogant attitude and by making changes achieved a great success in business.

8. GROWTH THROUGH PRODUCT CHOICE AND DEVELOPMENT

When I use the word 'product' it should be taken to also cover the provision of services. For the sake of simplicity if you own the right to sell something (time) then think of it as a PRODUCT. Even if it is your own time you are selling as a consultant it will be helpful to regard it as a product with all of its features and benefits well understood and defined.

Your time is probably the most valuable product you have. If you choose to rely on selling it, then it has two main constraints. Firstly, you cannot expand it, and secondly, time spent selling and bookkeeping can't itself be sold. It is essential not to under-price yourself if you are the actual product.

The equation of selling time, gets better as the scale increases. If you can employ say 10 people then one can do the selling, another do the accounts, with 8 having their time sold. Thus you can either reduce the price or make more profit. Small one-man consultancies are hard work.

After I retired and not wanting to be idle, I became an advisor to many companies. This was very interesting but not rewarding. There was a marked reluctance to pay me, firstly because they already knew

I was wealthy and were hoping for free advice. Secondly because my advice was usually so simple they felt they shouldn't pay a lot for it. They discounted the long, hard-working hours I had spent learning and understanding solutions to most problems.

I therefore for these reasons will from hereon in refer solely to PRODUCTS.

Your PRODUCT offering must offer clearly stated benefits to prospective customers. The importance of BENEFITS is very clearly explained in our companion book (*Cliff Clarifies the Business Basics*).

The first underpinning of growth (after people) is your range of product or products. Whether it is a consumer product, an industrial product, a component or capital item, it is only in very rare circumstances that it will not need improvements or replacing as time passes.

I recommend that all companies should have a policy of continual improvement. This should cover the product itself, the process by which it is made, and the way it is sold. I have been very surprised to note how many quite well-established companies have out-of-date or old-fashioned websites. Even mighty retailers such as TESCO or ASDA have been caught out by changes in their customers' behaviour. The increasing use of the internet, but more recently by mobile phone APPS, is revolutionising the way things are bought and sold.

Companies must urgently and routinely examine all aspects of their business. It is becoming obvious that the use of 3D printing is going to challenge large areas of the manufacturing world and even the medical profession. The appointment of young and enthusiastic product designers and developers is vital.

Reliance on product protection by patents, copyrights, etc., is becoming more problematic due to the speed that products are changed and marketing methods improved.

This product updating process should be a board level matter with Directors who understand the products, how they are made and sold. Too often financial matters are given a much higher priority. However, at the same time I found it valuable to train the technical staff in financial matters. This prevented the financial reporting system being used to bamboozle other directors. Too often financial considerations are basically short-term rather than strategic. Informed risk taking should be in the DNA of a well-run company. Eliminating risks too often results in a declining business which is unable to respond to new challenges.

1. FORECASTING

In my early days working for other companies as head of development I was required by non-technical directors; mostly financial or HR to forecast future sales. It was not well received when I replied that I did not know how many would be sold. Market research would help but for a totally new product the future was a mystery and risk, but if no changes were made there was a definite future – failure.

Thus, there should be a programme of continuing

market research allied to product and materials, research allied to invention in a documented plan. This plan should have expected time scales both for the development and sales processes with sustainable financial planning and production capabilities.

Hewlett Packard had a very insightful approach to these plans. They represented the company as a square. *Products, Facilities, Finances* and *People* were the four sides of the square. Strategic future plans were examined by this process. The forecast sales were used to define the lengths of the sides, which were: How many products were we to produce? How much production capacity did we need? How much money would we need? And finally, how many people to bring the plan to fruition?

All of these were derived from the sales forecasts and the consequential Business Plans developed by the various directors and managers.

The proposition was that the best results would be represented by a perfect square with all resources equally matched.

If one side of the square, say, 'production capacity' was shorter than the others, the resulting asymmetric quadrilateral would indicate that the plan would not succeed because there would be insufficient production capacity to meet the expected sales.

The other resources would be wasted by being too big for the eventual sales volume of the product. Efficient use of the company's resources would not happen and profit targets would be missed.

2. WAYS FORWARD

How then should you proceed to carry out this continual refreshment process? A good way forward is to use/copy the Japanese philosophy KAIZEN, which has become the name given to a process of continuous improvements. Some have taken this to recommend many small changes but in fact it also embraces large changes carried out by senior staff – the essential feature being continuous improvements in working practice by everyone in the company on an almost daily basis.

There is much written about this in books and on the internet. For me to repeat all of this would be counter-productive and as a consequence I recommend you read these articles yourself at times suitable to follow the advice which is widely published.

Article written for

South East Business Magazine, August 2003

THE ROLE OF INNOVATION IN COMPANY GROWTH

I continue to work with a variety of companies and organisations. Some of this work I hope will at some stage turn out to be of particular interest to you all and I will be able to write about it. In the meantime, however, I have come to the realisation that nearly all of the smaller companies and indeed some of the larger companies I have been talking to tend to have two specific problems that need addressing. These are

(1) **inadequate product development** and (2) **inadequate sales effort.**

Because of the inadequate product development and sales effort, the companies do not earn enough Gross Margin to be able to be profitable enough to keep re-investing in their own future and growth. Too many sit facing a relatively bleak future because of these two problems. Without doubt, to continue to develop product or services and at the same time invest in selling and make a living is an enormous challenge. However, that is the nature of business and if that is not cracked as a problem, then life continues to be quite difficult. As a result of these deliberations I have decided to devote the next two articles to these two subjects. This month's article will hopeful be some useful comments on **product development.**

For produce you can read services just as easily and certainly software development. I do not think wholly in terms of hardware product. When I first sat down to dictate this article I thought it would be a relatively straightforward process to unload my thoughts on this matter; in the event it has proved quite difficult. I have in the end decided to follow that old saying of 'who, what, why, when and where?' as my guiding headings for this process.

WHAT?

Essentially what you should develop falls into three specific categories. The first is the one that most people are bothered about, which is a *totally new product*. The second is completely *re-developing an older line*, and thirdly is just a *continuous process of updates and improvements of existing product*. Taking these in reverse order, **updates and improvements to existing product** should be a part of every company's attempt to remain competitive. I think that the problem is often that companies are so busy making their existing product that they cannot easily see where improvements can be made. Two ways to work with this problem is to check your competitors' products for features and advantages, and the second is perhaps to ask your own workforce or the people you know to do a critical appraisal of your product or process. The great advantage of small updates and improvements is that each one can be Press Released or Advertised and is a good reason to go back to your customers to keep them interested in your company which will form part of the sales process if it is also somewhat lacking.

The next heading of a complete **redevelopment** is where you have a product that is working quite well and has been continuously updated but needs to move into a new market, or where technology has moved ahead more quickly. These changes are often more obvious to the manufacturer but because of cost or other reasons (limited resources for example) the work just doesn't take place. Overall it is my impression that it is a lack of this continuous redevelopment of existing product ranges that is the underlying cause of lack of growth and success. Whilst small product updates and improvements keep you competitive they do not allow you to charge more from your customer, whereas complete redevelopments allow you to do so. As an example of this, just look at Microsoft. They have continuously updated varieties of Windows and charged all of us huge sums of money to make certain we stay up-to-date. The same principles are applicable to most people's products.

Finally we come to **totally new products**. I sometimes think there is too big an obsession with totally new products but without doubt they are the strongest way forward for larger growth in companies. However, you do not necessarily have to have a strong programme of in-house Research and Development, although that of course does give you control over your intellectual property. The other ways to do it are to license a product from somebody else, to buy in from somebody else, to copy and improve somebody else (which is an underrated pastime) and finally maybe to develop a product in conjunction with another company. Each of these methodologies is worth considerable thought as they can be extremely cost-effective and speedy ways of moving a company forward. It was certainly the process I used to build Densitron.

WHY?

There really is only one serious answer to why you should carry out innovative development, because if you don't you will die. Without doubt that is the fate awaiting people who do not redevelop their product range. It might take years; it may even take as long as 20 years, but die you will because some competitor will come along with something better or newer. So in that, SURVIVAL is the number one rule for any one company – you need to develop or die. However, you can also do it not just to defend a position but also to aggressively grow your company, and that is possibly the best way forward for a sane and secure future.

When Densitron was a private company, I would from time to time gamble up to 50% of the company's previous year's profits on new ventures. When it became a public company, I cut this back to something in the region of 25% of past year's profits to be spent on trying to grow and improve the company. I felt, as a private company where only my own wealth was at stake, it was legitimate to be more aggressive than where people were investing their savings in the public company. I am not entirely certain that was a totally valid decision because it was a more defensive position that I had taken using my own money, but that is what I did.

Finally, you could do a new product development just because you like it, and there is nothing wrong with that because very often an obsession with a product or an idea can completely transform a company.

WHEN?

The answer to this heading is absolutely clear and is answered in only one word: **'continuously'**. Product improvement development should be continuous. To try to do it in stops and starts or with a variety of specialised programmes is always a mistake. Product development, product improvement, and change should be at the heart of every company if you wish to SURVIVE, GROW, and be PROFITABLE. If you don't want to be those three things then of course it isn't quite so important. I should like to reassure you that it isn't all that difficult to carry it out continuously. Time should be taken out of your busy schedule. Even maybe 30 minutes at the beginning of each week on a Monday to sit down and say, "What shall we do new this week?" would make a tremendous difference. Too often the immediate pressures are overly burdensome and no time is given to thinking about the future.

Some many years ago I learned a wise saying that I would pass on to you, and that is to understand the difference between **importance** and **urgency**. A thing can be important but not urgent, and a thing can be urgent but not important.

The ability to understand the ramifications of the use of these two words is of course vital to every business. You have to do those things too often which are both urgent and important, which detracts from that which is important but not urgent. It is here that I feel time management can play its full part. Product development seems not to be an urgent matter but it certainly is important, therefore it would pay to put some time aside to deal with it even when everything else seems more urgent. I commend this thought to you very strongly.

WHO?

This conundrum was partly answered in the first section. You should use whoever produces the results quickest and most competitively. Using your own in-house staff is certainly the most secure thing to do. It is also without doubt the most costly. It takes a long time to find outstanding development engineers or development personnel, and they are hard to replace if you need to do so. The biggest advantage that they have is, of course, that you own the intellectual property which they generate, but more importantly you can use them in the general running of your company. I think the old model that Britain had of an R&D department in an ivory tower, separate from the rest of the company, was sadly mistaken. It is certainly where I spent 12 happy years of my life, but when I look back at the products I developed at that time, I am not convinced they brought much prosperity to the companies. I think that the Engineering and Sales teams should be very closely allied to production and if at all possible they should be managed as a complete entity. There is no reason at all why production people cannot suggest the continuous improvements necessary or indeed implement them. They can also often suggest to sales, features and advantages which they may not have identified. Similarly, a good discussion going on between sales development in conjunction with production will help ensure that no product reaches production that is impossible or too expensive to produce. At the end of the day the whole process is designed to make a profit, and if the product is overly clever or difficult to sell or difficult to make, then the company cannot prosper. By using all of those three departments working together in conjunction with, if I may dare say so, an enlightened and progressive-thinking Accounts Department, then you can be on to sure-fire winners. The accounting costing process should be integral to the whole structure and this is where they have their greatest advantage to forward-thinking companies. If accounting is just used as a controlling or reporting function, you're missing the process of doing forward calculations in a positive manner. I know I have banged on long and hard over the years about accountants, but this is the area where they should put in positive input, not to control product development but to enhance and speed it up.

We finally come to: WHERE?

It really doesn't matter where you do your new product development, although from the paragraphs above it is plain that it is very powerful if it is done inside the company as a process of teamwork. However, there is no reason why you cannot use people in other companies to do the work for you provided they benefit from it from receiving orders. There is no reason at all why you cannot use consultants or advisers and wacky inventors. The important thing is that you do continuously improve your product range and that those improvements are brought to the attention of your customers and sold aggressively.

These days with the dominance of the Worldwide Web, product development can take place virtually anywhere in the world and you can shop around to find an effective partner around the globe. This is possible now even for the smallest of companies, particularly if they are fortunate enough to live in a broadband area.

SUMMARY

Product improvement and development is the engine room of all companies whether they are financial services companies, software companies, or manufacturing companies. Allowing your product line to age produces pseudo-profits in the short-term but ultimately will kill your company. The only time realistically to cut back on product development and rely on extra profits generated is when you want to sell the company, then you just have to pray that those people wishing to buy the company don't spot your subterfuge.

I hope these random thoughts and suggestions are of some value to you.

***

3. INCREASE INTELLECTUAL PROPERTY (R&D)

Intellectual property covers the protection of your products or writings by a variety of methods. These are dealt with quite fully in my companion book about business basics. Here I am considering the positive and negative aspects of these procedures. The first one that springs to most people's mind is gaining a *patent*.

4. PATENTS

It is worth mentioning that you have to patent in all of the territories that you wish to protect. This can be costly for a smaller company.

Patents are granted by the patent office and there are quite demanding criteria which will take up quite a lot of your time. They are also expensive to get approved and maintain. The advantage they bring is that if approved, they can prevent others copying your work, thus allowing you to improve your financial returns.

There are, however, some significant negatives other than complexity and cost. The first is that your patent will be published together with any drawings and production processes involved in its creation. This allows competitors to examine it and see if they can get round its claims without infringing the actual patent. More aggressively, they can copy it, in which case you will have to take them to court for damages and to implement your rights for protection. If you don't have the money for this, "YOU LOSE," and your patent is worthless. Some people claim that a patent is only strong when it has been challenged in court and won. Patents are powerful but they expire 25 years from their registration. This will be very relevant if it takes a long time to get into meaningful production. The drugs industry has a particular problem caused by the long time taken by field trials. Sometimes they may only have very short time for profitable sales before the patent expires and others can copy without all the costs of invention and trials.

5. COPYRIGHT

Personally I found that claiming copyright was quite a powerful protection. Copyright not only covers books but almost any original writing (music) and very importantly, drawings and images. The copyright comes into force when the writing or drawing is done. It is vital that if you are seeking to claim copyright that you clearly date the items involved together with a name.

I learnt a very hard lesson myself when I imported some quite mechanically advanced digital displays from an excellent Japanese company who had devised the clever mechanics. I was convinced that a large market was available and approached the advertising and sale very aggressively. I had to buy a significant initial stock to get a world exclusive for it sales.

Imagine my shock in getting a letter from an American company saying that we infringed their copyright. I wrote back pointing out that the two displays were made by two different technologies. The Americans in turn replied by pointing out that their copyright lay in the particular shapes of the segments rather than the technology used in their manufacture.

I challenged this but that was when I found out the power of a dated copyright. Aware of the importance of dating, I asked them to prove their claim by sending a copy of the drawings. Their reply was that if I wanted to see the dates then I would see them when they sued us for infringement in an American court. They didn't have to prove that they had copyright but would sue us if we continued with our sales efforts.

Prudently I chose not to challenge them in an American court. If I had lost the costs would have been very large and compounded by the write-off of the stock. In this way you can get some sense of the protection available through the copyright laws. They can also be valid for much longer than a patent. I used copyright claims on many occasions when we were larger and with stronger finances. I found that I could challenge others in the way we had been challenged. Most people backed down. We carefully dated important writings and drawings ever after. Sometimes some small but significant changes to shapes and software gained us big orders. As we sourced many products from Asia we always altered the shapes and the controlling software so that we could frighten others with our claims for copyright. Few challenged us due to the legal costs and the fear of paying compensation.

Other forms of intellectual property protection are in registered designs and trademarks, and are worth researching on the internet for the protection they offer.

In summary, the great benefit of *intellectual property* is that it gives you a protected market. The negatives are uncertainty, delays, and cost. Use with care.

Many times it will be better to exploit a market opportunity quickly and then move on to improved or changed products.

6. TRADEMARKS

A trademark distinguishes products or services from a particular source. It is usually a recognisable sign or expression drawn in a particular way.

7. INDUSTRIAL DESIGN

This right protects the visual appearance of a product that is not just utilitarian. It can comprise shape, colour, pattern, and other similar features. Once again, expert advice is essential.

8. TRADE DRESS AND TRADE SECRETS

These are less widely used and I once again recommend going to an expert.

In summary, there are a range of tools available to enable you to protect your business; its name; its products and inventions, etc. The purpose of using these is to enable you to get the maximum benefit from running your business for the maximum duration of time. It is a complex area of law and my comments are only a guide as to the range of protection available, and you should seek expert advice at an early stage. Your protection will only be as good as your ability to finance a defence of your rights. Small companies will be at a severe disadvantage against much larger ones. In these circumstances an alliance with a friendly company by way of a licence may be a good way forward.

Adding new products or new versions is the best and safest way to grow.

9. OTHER GROWTH CREATORS

Most of these act more quickly than a new product.

What are the other main growth drivers?
1) Sell more to existing customers
2) Attract new customers
3) Expand geographic area
4) Develop technical excellence
5) Acquire an existing range from another company
6) Acquire another company
7) Merge with another enterprise
8) Use of Market Research

1. SELL MORE TO EXISTING CUSTOMERS!

This is often the easiest way to increase sales. Mostly this will be achieved by the regular sales routes. If your customer is in retail, do they have other locations or departments? Will a special offer create more sales? Can you get a bigger percentage of the whole order? It will repay thought expended in a brainstorming session.

2. ATTRACT NEW CUSTOMERS

This will use all of your sales abilities to get noticed and have an attractive offer. Your website is vital and should be reviewed regularly by senior staff to check it is up-to-date and easy to use. It is important to remember that *your* website must be attractive and informative to potential new customers. The problem is, how do they find your website amongst all of the huge number of competitors?

The answer is to drive customers to your site by other routes such as Facebook and Twitter or even old-fashioned methods such as press advertising and catalogue distribution by mail. This latter method has grown dramatically in recent years. Going to exhibitions can work for specialised products. Writing articles for papers and magazines is powerful if you can write them. If not, get someone else to write articles about your ideas, but get into relevant publications.

You can pay Google or do 'AdWords' but these can be expensive for smaller companies. At the end of the day it is dependent upon the quality of your imagination and the work you put into finding the right route.

One area that is often neglected is ensuring that your response to an enquiry is first class. Too many times a phone is left ringing or inadequate information left on the website. Just this morning as I am writing this part of the book I have had an example of a careless and inadequate response. I phoned an agent with an enquiry about a £400,000 commercial property. They had dealt with it before, about two years ago. I rang the nearest branch and was answered by a very new and young person. They spent some time getting all my details and then put me on hold whilst they talked to a more senior person. When she came back it turned out that the information I needed was now transferred to a different location. They undertook to alert the staff at the new location who would contact me. I explained that I would only be here until mid-day and would not be at work again for a day. I waited and waited but as the matter was quite urgent I ultimately phoned the new location directly myself. I explained my problem all over again, which it turned out they had received, and was transferred to the right department. Unfortunately the person I needed to talk to was out with a client but I would be contacted on his return. I am still waiting. In this day of easy instant communication, surely someone should alert him to call me with an acknowledgement of his interest. They are plainly more concerned with their own agenda rather than the needs of gaining a customer through good service.

In summary it is probably good to refer to advice I got in JAPAN. I was once told there that the customer is not King, he is God. Not a bad piece of guidance.

Another way to approach new customers is by doing online sales. Even if you have a catalogue and a great website, new customers can be attracted by an online sales service. If you are big enough then there are companies who will develop an online shop for you. Alternatively you can sell through Amazon or others whilst still retaining your Brand.

3. EXPAND YOUR GEOGRAPHIC SALES AREA

Inevitably when a new company is created its main customer base is likely to be relatively local. Ultimately this will be limiting to your sales volume and it will be pertinent to consider expanding into new geographic areas. Fortunately there is a very wide range of ways to do this. The important point is not to try to do too many at once.

Do some internet-based market research to identify potential new customers and draw a map of an expanded area with these potential new customers clearly marked, and with the potential size indicated.

Next, prioritise them in a list that includes paying attention to distance, potential size, and any advantages with contacts or product benefits you can think of. Then approach just one to find out the best contacts and try to arrange a meeting. You should use the phone and surface mail as well as emails. The problem with using just emails is that yours can be swamped out on any particular day and effectively fall off the bottom of the page, so to speak. The first approach should aim at getting a face-to-face conversation. This is best done by identifying the person to meet and then trying to make an attractive and interesting offer dependent upon a meeting.

I stress that you should at first try out your ideas and techniques on potential customers one at a time.

By doing the approaches one at a time you limit the damage that an inadequate proposition makes, and thus steadily improve your approach. When you have refined your offer and are getting new business then expand your activities to a wider and larger area. By extension it follows that your first attempts should be on smaller opportunities nearer to your base, leaving the bigger opportunities for when you have refined your approach.

MY SIMPLE APPROACH TO GROWTH BASED ON TECHNICAL EXCELLENCE AND INNOVATION.

This was the basis of the whole of the outstanding growth and profitability of my company, Densitron, for most of its existence. We basically bought product from larger manufacturers but had the standard product modified through our own design teams. Our company motto was **N**ovel **E**ngineering **W**orldwide **S**olutions. These four words described our sales intentions. We produced innovative products and made them available all around the world. We even claimed to be open for business 365 days a year, 24 hrs a day. We had so many locations with differing work patterns that this was true. We had subsidiaries in all major time zones and as Japan did not celebrate Christmas at that time our claims were true.

EXAMPLE 1

An example of our methods: we at one time had an enquiry from a major Scandinavian manufacturer for a large number of LCD alphanumeric displays. Our source was Sanyo, where we had a very close long-term arrangement with the specific factory making a part that met the basic specification. The parent Sanyo company had a trading subsidiary that we had to compete with in the open market around the world. This large order was going to attract them and all other large manufacturers. We discussed the requirement with the customer's own design engineers and learnt that they had used standard displays in the prototype but were not satisfied with their readability. We set out to remedy this and succeeded in doing so by modifying the software that controlled the display. We didn't tell them this or let our supplier know either. All the competitors concentrated on cost and we got the order at a 30% higher price. Even when Sanyo's sales arm told the customer that they were our supplier and offered a 20% lower price. We retained the business because they could not match our level of clarity. Our attention to customers' requirements earned us this business for many years.

EXAMPLE 2

Another occasion was in the UK, where a well-known manufacturer was intending to create a new product using a high-resolution quarter VGA monochrome graphic display. Price on this occasion was a defining requirement. The customer wanted around 4,000 units for the first order but unfortunately nobody at all made monochrome displays in this size, they were all colour. This company thought that 4,000 units was a large order; most factories were making 40,000 units a month, so 4,000 specials was not much of an attraction.

We won this business by doing a special deal with a new manufacturer for a one-time order for 4,000 of the colour displays having the right characteristics. We then turned off the colour software, making it a very competitive monochrome display.

We negotiated the supply of prototypes to be supplied only after we had a guaranteed order for 4,000 units secured by an irrevocable Letter of Credit for the whole amount. This to be activated by the delivery of working prototypes. We knew that the customer's engineers would spot what we had done and get another supplier to make them. The irrevocable LoC prevented this. We only got two orders but this was several million pounds and we were happy.

In summary, therefore, expanding your geographic territory if properly managed will bring the much-needed opportunity for growth. However, it will also bring significant management and competitive challenges. Your ability to meet these challenges with organising ability welded to innovative products will determine whether you get continuing good results. It will certainly require you to recruit and train top-class people.

4. ACQUIRE A NEW PRODUCT RANGE BY BUYING ONE FROM ANOTHER COMPANY

Sometimes companies will decide to close a division or to exit a given product area. Buying such a range of products can be a good way to grow quickly. The problem is that such chances only occur randomly and can be difficult to spot. Constant awareness and a policy to deal with any opportunity will repay itself. Careful consideration of this idea and laying down some guidelines can help you react quickly and get a bargain. I never used this mechanism myself but I did sell some product ranges we did not wish to follow.

EXAMPLE

A specific example of this occurred in the first five years of my company when it was still private. We had had a lot of success in the consumer home HiFi audio marketplace. In particular we sold a bookshelf speaker called the Minimax11 manufactured in Hungary.

In my early days, 1955-60, when working for Mullards (part of Phillips) I had been responsible for designing new high-quality amplifiers using Mullard Thermionic valves. Transistors were only just being introduced. As a result I was well versed in audio products and when I heard this speaker I took a chance to sell under the brand name '*Videotone*'. The Hungarian company was named 'Videoton' and employed around 40,000 people in producing a wide range of electronic products, of which the speaker was a small part. The great advantage I had was that the Hungarians were only interested in employment and production and did not understand value. As a consequence we paid a very low price for what was a world-beating product and made a huge margin selling it into England.

Despite this I did not enjoy how the consumer market operated at that time and after a few years of success I decided to sell the range to another company. They got a bargain and I got some much-needed liquidity to help our growth into the industrial electronics industry. This turned out to be a very good decision and we continued to source from Hungary a wider range of products including computer terminals. This was a very good decision because it concentrated our efforts into diverse but similar markets, allowing the development of simpler financial and managing structures. As said earlier, I never had an occasion to buy a product range but I did buy and or merge with other companies for strategic reasons.

5. ACQUIRING AN EXISTING COMPANY

I did this several times to take advantage of others' difficulties and to get quick expansion. This mostly happened in the early days before the major consolidation that happened at flotation in 1986.

EXAMPLE

In fact the first acquisition was to buy an existing manufacturing company owned and run by one of my first investors. The company was called RBS Capacitors Ltd and made high-quality Mica capacitors mostly for the industrial market, with small amounts to the TV manufacturers. This happened in my first year of operation, 1972. It was owned by a sensible businessman named George Lee who had inherited the company from its original three founders. Renshaw, Broderick, and Stringer (hence RBS). George was a talented moving picture cameraman but knew little about electronics. He was a friend of the Managing Director of Hewlett Packard UK, Dennis Taylor, who wished to invest in my new venture. He in turn introduced John Penrose who was the HP UK Finance Director. These were my first three partners. The difference between them and me was that they all had jobs with regular income and I didn't.

To solve these problems altogether in a simple way, we created a *holding company* which was ultimately to own all our ventures; it was named Taylor Miller (TM).

It owned my first two companies, Perdix Components, an importing sales company, and the speaker importer Videotone. Ownership of these two was easy because they were start-ups and effectively had no market value. Integrating RBS was more difficult because it had been going some time and had profits and value.

It was decided to do two things. One was to have

me employed by RBS as Sales Director with a regular salary, and then to acquire the company to be one third of TM. To do this we borrowed the money from our bank (and HP's) which was much easier done in those days, especially when a major customer such as HP was involved. The money was secured by the value of RBS and a charge over all the company's assets.

At this stage TM's shareholders were: me with 31%, George Lee with 20%, Dennis Taylor with 30%, and John Penrose with 19%. In this way the two working members, George and I, controlled the company with 51% of the shares. This was at the insistence of George who felt that we two had the most to lose; in this he was dead right, and later on this structure proved vital to me.

RBS was our first acquisition and cost us £36,000. Some years later I sold it for around £400,000. Acting as a Marketing and Sales Director I had increased the sales and profits dramatically. Before my involvement they had had no dedicated sales effort. It supported the whole venture for some long time before we sold it. What was important in this story was that we knew that there was a viable market to attack and that we had the expertise and money to attack it.

6. HOW WE GOT A HIGH PRICE IN SELLING RBS

There were two main competitors but they had many other product ranges to keep them occupied. When we came to sell RBS we played these two competitors against each other, as our market share was significant and whoever got us would dominate the marketplace. We managed to convince each of them in turn that the other was offering a higher price, which was not the actual case. But they kept increasing their offers to prevent the other winning.

ANOTHER EXAMPLE

The next acquisition was a different story and involved chance, luck, and quick thinking. Whilst employed as a technical salesman by HP I had a customer named Nore Microwave who were a small subsidiary of a much larger American-controlled company. They bought surprisingly large amounts of high-priced measuring equipment from us but would not allow me to know why. Their main product ranges in no way required such advanced equipment. All I could find out was that it was used for military purposes. It was many years after leaving HP that I found out they made equipment used for calibrating the accuracy of ground RADAR systems.

Shortly after starting TM and acquiring RBS I was approached by Nore Microwave's American owners to see if I would like to be interviewed for the post of European Sales Manager covering all their products. I wasn't really interested but was egotistical enough to see if I could get an offer.

During the interview I asked them what they intended to do with Nore Microwave as it didn't seem to fit in with their plans. They had elected to close it down and when I said that seemed a pity they asked me if I would like to buy it! I replied that I was interested but would have to discuss it with my partners. They agreed for me to do this and eventually we made an offer of £30,000 for the whole company and its customers.

It was decided for status reasons that Dennis (MD of HP) should meet with the American European MD. It turned out he felt that if such an eminent person as Dennis was involved there must be some secret product or business contained in Nore and we were trying to get it cheaply. As Dennis knew nothing about Nore he was unable to complete the deal. It was then decided that I should meet the American to discuss it more fully. We met at the Dorchester for lunch and I found out their worries. I went through all the reasons we wanted to buy such a small company. I wrote in my diary a statement that there was definitely no secret product or knowledge. It was just that Nore suited our size of business and our knowledge base. I dated and signed this statement, tore the two pages out of my diary, and gave them to him after having them photocopied. The statement was true but we were able to grow the company, and in around 2000 sold it for £8m using the same competition issues as in the RBS situation.

Again, some lateral thinking gained us this huge sum.

7. MISTAKES AND FAILURE IN ACQUISITIONS

There were a couple of successes, but one acquisition venture went very wrong and nearly put us out of business.

It was at a time when we were selling very high volumes of the Minimax11 bookshelf speakers. We were approached by two men who owned and ran a consumer electronics company mostly involved with music centres, which were very popular at that time. They were in their mid-sixties and wishing to retire, but had the chance of a large continuing order for music centre modules for a large German company. They offered to sell their company to us for £1 if we took on the financing of this order and ran the company into the future.

My financial partner (FD of HP) carried out a due diligence check on the books and the impact this deal would have on our venture. He gave it a clean bill of health and recommended us to go ahead. I didn't realise at this time he had no experience of this type of activity.

The next move was to visit the new company's bank to see about financing the deal. We needed to borrow some £400k to buy the components. The bank was the NatWest in the city. The manager listened to our story and confirmed that they would happily finance the order, but with two caveats.

We should get the order placed in US dollars, but also with a confirmed Letter of Credit for the whole amount covering all of the order. On the basis of this we went ahead with taking over the company. I then flew out to Germany with one of the original directors and negotiated the order on the terms dictated by the bank. The Germans were not happy but in the end placed the order with the Letter of Credit in US Dollars as required by the bank. I returned to England ecstatic at this success.

I went to see the bank manager to report our achievement and arrange for the loan. The bank manager was fulsome in his praise. He stated that if more English businessmen were like me, got up off their arses and went out to get export orders, the country would solve all its economic problems.

Feeling very happy, I asked to negotiate the terms of the loan and this is where NatWest lived up to the finest traditions of British banking. The manager asked for our collateral against the order. I replied that we had met his terms and got an irrevocable LoC for the full amount. "Ah," he said, "but what happens if you don't deliver the product?" Effectively the bank was not going to lend us the money other than against tradable assets for the full amount. We were sunk.

By this time we had taken over the company and were managing it. We found that there were masses of hidden unpaid invoices not entered in to the books and an overstated stock position, plus some sizeable bad debts. None of this had been uncovered by our FD accountant. A quick calculation showed we were insolvent and we had to turn to our original bank. They were prepared to support us but only against a charge over our homes. We had no choice but to accept this offer. We closed down the acquisition and ran our existing business as hard and economically as we could until we had paid back the new loan.

Eventually this led to another shock. Our bank would not cancel the charges over our houses until the company was in a zero debt position with them. We only achieved this after floating the company in 1986, some 10 years later. Even then they tried to keep control of our houses, but we refused.

At one stage the government were trying to improve the service that British banks gave to our industries. I wrote to the *Sunday Times* about it and was published. This led to several interesting developments and some extra publicity for the firm and myself. Ultimately I ended up on a television programme about 'Bad Practice by Banks'.

What are the lessons from this episode?

1) Make certain you do really effective due diligence.

2) Check out a bank offer very fully.

3) Only allow a charge over your house in extremis.

4) Only take over businesses which you fully understand and where you bring in an extra dimension.

5) If the price seems low then something will be wrong.

Acquisitions can be a good way to create growth but beware of the details and take great care. A good company will only be offered at a 'highish' price, which means getting a large return will be difficult. A bad company will be cheap but it will still be a bad company.

> **The golden rule for an acquisition is that you must understand it and know how to integrate it into your organisation with outstanding opportunities.**

When I first joined HP they had been through a cycle of several acquisitions. All of them had difficulties and HP had to put its own management teams into them. It was HP's opinion that it is better to start a new company yourself than acquire a company in difficulties. I should have listened.

8. MERGE WITH ANOTHER COMPANY

As an alternative to acquisition there is the possibility of merging with another company.

Merging means that two (or more) independent companies agree to become *one* under a common name and ownership. This is different to an acquisition where normally the acquired company remains a separately managed entity but its shares are held by the acquiring company.

In the merging process it is relatively simple to deal with the financial arrangements that will be in place after the merger. Obviously shareholders will be the controlling feature as there will have to be proper majorities agreeing to the new arrangement. The rules will be as laid out in the Memorandum and Articles of Association. Proper legal advice is essential. The new entity will have new shares and the shareholders may be different to the original ones in deciding to take cash instead of new shares.

The greatest difficulty is normally agreeing the management structure. There will have been two Boards of Directors and two separate management structures. In merging there will be seen to be winners and losers, as there will need to be only one Board and one management structure. Negotiating these changes will be better arranged before the merger rather than later. The biggest challenge will be at the Board level where there is more to gain and lose combined with significant egos.

Merging two companies where there is a large difference in size is easier to negotiate. Where there are two larger companies with comparable sizes, there will be more difficulty. Ultimately the shareholders have the final say but powerful directors with a large salary at stake can prove difficult to control. It pays not to fudge the issue of a director being appointed against the wishes of another. A company needs a single voice with little to no conflict between the Chairman and the CEO. The more specialist roles such as HR or technical directors usually cause smaller problems.

EXAMPLE

The only real merger I was involved in was the creation of Densitron International Ltd which occurred immediately before its flotation on June 5th 1986.

This was a really complex sequence of legal steps. At its heart was the merging of my company, Taylor Miller Ltd ('TM'), with Mr Degawa's company, Densitron Japan ('DCJ'). He had the larger revenues and little profit. I had lots of assets and was more profitable. He had a significant subsidiary in Los Angeles, California, 'DCA' run by a very talented individual, Keith Luskin. DCJ had several small outside shareholders.

TM Ltd by that time had two large outside shareholders owning 29% between them and several wholly owned subsidiaries with also two separate spin-outs with independent shareholders who wished to join in the flotation.

We had to invent the new structure and determine the values of each shareholding in each company. There was almost complete agreement between myself, Degawa, and Keith Luskin, who were to be the main drivers of the combined entity. The biggest problem came from the two major shareholders in TM who wanted to remain as shareholders after flotation. For a variety of reasons this could not be accommodated and they had to be bought out. These negotiations took a long time but finally they accepted £350,000 each. They had originally invested £3,000 so it wasn't a bad return. It should be noted that without their help none of this success would have happened so I do not begrudge their reward. The largest investing original shareholder I had was the MD of HP Dennis Taylor. He had sold out to me years earlier for £60,000.

Our lawyers and accountants had to value and organise all this work, which at one time involved a sequence of some 25 shareholder and Board meetings held on one day, with about 10 minutes between each meeting. Our advisers certainly earned their money and their expertise really impressed me. Ultimately we created a new holding company, '*Densitron International Ltd* ('DIL'), which held appropriate shareholdings in the various companies. We made nearly everyone a shareholder who had been in the company, in a senior role, for over 10 years. This turned out to be something of a mistake as several new American shareholders sold them immediately and took the cash. All Japanese and Europeans held on to theirs for the long term. Many of these, including Mr Degawa, won big time in the dot-com boom.

At flotation we were valued at £10,000,000 with me holding 31% for my initial investment of £3,500.

What are the main issues to consider in approaching a merger?

Without doubt the prime consideration must be that it is being done for positive reasons. Some mergers are done in order to save a failing company. It is my opinion that these should be regarded as takeovers even if technically they are a merger.

The reason for these words of caution is because a good merger benefits both sides. Not necessarily equally due to reasons of size or technology, etc., but because all participants feel they are better off afterwards than continuing alone.

As indicated at the beginning of this section it will almost certainly be the people issues that are the trickiest to resolve in satisfying feelings of fairness. If there are senior people who cannot be reconciled to the common cause they should be made to move on elsewhere. As the saying goes, '*a whole barrel of apples will be spoilt by one rotten one*'.

It can be helpful to create a guidebook which details the various rules and guidelines by which the new enterprise will be managed. This provision of a common set of guidelines is a very valuable provision and should be treated with great respect. It mustn't be either bureaucratic or lightweight and leave plenty of room for personal decision making. This guidebook, when combined with the idea of corporate objectives dealt with elsewhere, provides a strong trunk for the whole tree of the enterprise to prosper. An example of the guidebook used at one time in Densitron is given as an addendum to this book.

9. MARKET RESEARCH IDEAS

It is essential that you use market research as much as possible. I am not suggesting expensive consultants to do this, but rather you use your intelligence and existing resources to inform you.

One example I can give you is when I was working for an electronic component manufacturer where a large proportion of the output went to the rapidly expanding television set manufacturers (before the Asian invasion). One of our problems was that we didn't have any idea what share of the market we had from each of the major set manufacturers, and naturally they wouldn't tell us.

In my role as Technical Marketing Manager I devised 'a cunning plan'. I visited several local retail outlets and gave them money to let me open each of the various TV sets, and then counted how many of our type of components they were using and how many came from us and how many from our competitors. After some months of this activity we had a very good idea of our share of the market and what new competitors (both technically and commercially) were appearing. This was an accurate, simple, and low-cost exercise.

Whilst at the same company there arose another challenge. At that time there was a very successful electronic manufacturer by the name of Elliot Brothers. They had several large locations but operated as a conglomeration of smallish divisions all operating independently at these locations.

Our problem was that we had no business with this company and by and large had no idea what they built. We had to find out whether we could get any business from them. My Sales Director got me to go to each location and not return until I had visited every division and met either the Buyer or Chief Engineer. I had a few contacts but certainly not enough. I made appointments to meet with these contacts so that I had a reason to visit the location. I would show a great deal of interest in the work of my contact but at the same time I would get as much information about the other divisions as I could without causing offence.

I found that each division had four main managers which were (1) the Chief Design Engineer, (2) the Buyer, (3) the Production Manager, and (4) the

Component Standardisation Engineer, who tried to work with colleagues in the other divisions to limit the range of suppliers they bought from. This was quite a problem because each chief engineer worked independently.

I developed a plan which was to use the component standardisation engineers to pass me on to their colleagues in other divisions to help them in their work. My wide personal experience as a design engineer allowed me to be very helpful. I knew a lot about other component manufacturers and could give help and advice to each division on other products than our own. I became very welcome.

After the standards engineer I talked to the production manager to find out what problems he had with using the various components in the design. In those days there was limited discussion between the various departments as each manager sought to defend his territory. I behaved as a very sympathetic and knowledgeable friend to each person.

From production I moved to the chief engineer, where in discussing our products I was able to indicate the problems that the Standards and Production engineers had. I tried to suggest solutions even if they didn't involve our products. Finally I would meet with the buyer who was almost always obsessed with price. I was able to use by now my wide knowledge to discuss other problems and thus reduce to focus on price.

Even doing this, I could not reach every division, but got lucky. Between each meeting I had to return to the front security gate and as a result became quite friendly with the security guards. They became interested in why I was spending so much time at their location (on occasions it took several days to meet everyone). It turned out they had a complete directory of all the staff, their title, and their internal phone numbers. They allowed me to use this to call each relevant person and introduce myself. I used the names of the people already met, inferring that they had recommended that I should visit this particular individual because of his importance and work.

In the end I had visited all the relevant people at all locations. I knew what they made and what components they used in what quantities. I even had ideas on how to improve our packing to facilitate their stores procedures.

All this took some five weeks, during which time I obeyed my instructions not to return until I had been to all locations and found out all relevant contact and technical details.

When first given this task and the accompanying directions I thought it was a stupid waste of time. But our sales increased and we developed a series of new products. My director was himself surprised because he had not realised the scale of the task he had set me and initially thought I was skiving off, using the task as an excuse to stay at home.

10. MARKET RESEARCH LESSONS

What are the lessons I am trying to pass on with these two stories? Essentially it is that market research is vital and rewarding. You can be quite inventive about how to get it done. A subsidiary point is that it can be OK to make small mistakes in starting new ventures as long as you learn from them before approaching the larger players.

11. GROW GEOGRAPHICALLY

The underlying problem with expanding your geographic reach is how to manage this larger territory. If you can do it yourself from existing locations then that is the best way forward. Depending on your business model it may need your salesmen to be located around the larger area and probably working from home. This is a very regularly used solution but has administrative and motivational difficulties. If your sales force exceeds 10 in number you may well find that you have to split the whole territory into specific regions, each with at least 4 salesmen and a regional manager. Trying to manage more than 6 salesmen directly becomes a difficult proposition and a lack of focus.

Ultimately you may find you need regional offices, which have considerable cost implications. The closer proximity to your customer base must be able to absorb these extra costs and still increase profits. The main driver behind such regional structures will be the need to visit your customers, regularly updating them and asking for increased orders. The other dimension is of course the need to compete against other potential suppliers. Your sales force should not only be able to solicit for business but be an excellent source of information about your customer base and the nature of the competition. This live feedback is very fertile ground for new product ideas or directions. One big caveat, however, is that your competition will probably be getting the same feedback and therefore you could all end up with the same range of products or services. This should be resisted by your own design innovations, giving you a competitive edge. It may be that you solve the same customer problem but do it in a different way to your competitors.

10. UNDERSTAND YOUR RESOURCES

SUMMARY OF THE MAIN RESOURCES

There is almost an unending list of resources but it will simplify the discussion if we consider first the four main ones. These are PEOPLE, PRODUCTS, MONEY, and PREMISES. I choose these as the main ones based upon the various opinions expressed earlier in the book.

My first suggestion is to consider these four resources as inextricably linked in the following way.

Draw a square and label each side of the square with one of the four resources. The centre section of the square can be regarded as indicating your potential sales volume. Then consider whether all these four sides are equal. If they are not then you will have a misshapen quadrilateral rather than a square. This indicates inefficiency and lost sales. You will need a very accurate understanding of the relationships between these resources to get value out of this idea. You will need to know how much premises space you need to make and/or store your products. You will need to have an outstanding management capability to decide how many people you need (not want) for a given volume of sales.

With regard to products, you will have to be aware of items being in stock for long periods which can be a good indicator of an inadequate design or sales effort. Alternatively if you have unreasonable delays in delivery it can indicate lack of production or money to expand production.

Finally, the thorniest problem of all is money. How much do you need and where should it be spent? There are two main uses for money in an enterprise.

One is for capital expenditure on fixed assets such as property, machinery, R&D, patents, and to some extent, staff. This money can only be released by selling the asset or borrowing against it.

The other main use is in working capital. That is money used in a cyclical way in making products, paying staff, paying suppliers, advertising, carrying stock, financing credit given to customers, etc. These issues are dealt with in a following section on financial planning.

What are the limits to the supply of these assets?

People

As already discussed, people are your most valuable asset; attracting them and keeping them becomes of prime importance. Unfortunately there is no single provision that solves these problems. As indicated earlier you should try to recruit the very best people you can afford and then manage them by objectives. How well you are able to recruit staff, manage and reward them will be dependent upon your personality and management skills, together with a good company image and money for salaries. These lead to an almost impossibly complex set of employment equations. Solving these equations is the key to successfully growing your company.

There are several steps in growing the number of people you employ. The biggest is your first one. When you start your company you are probably alone. The recruitment of your first employee is a 100% increase in your company staff. When there are ten of you an extra person is an increase of 10% and with a hundred a 1% increase, and so on and on.

Increasing staff allows for more specialisation and you grow from employing generalists to employing specialists such as accountants, engineers, HR managers. Increased specialisation should increase efficiency but it requires a first-class management structure, adequate finance and clear objectives.

It is my opinion that a company reaches the beginning of successful growth when it can create a meaningful Board of Directors. I firmly believe that the creation of an effective Board is an essential step in creating and sustaining profitable growth. Even if they are non-executive and part-time directors, good advice is invaluable.

In the many years I spent advising other companies how to grow, it was my experience that few, if any, were prepared to share power in a Board of Directors. Surprisingly the main resource ignored was a Finance Director. Almost all of the companies that failed to grow profitably or even fail totally were because of inadequate internal financial advice. It is vital that you not only have this internal advice but that you understand it. It is equally wrong to just accept an internal accountant's advice as it is not to have any. I have tried to advise many very capable companies who without a proper understanding of costs and cash flow got into deep difficulties. Some became insolvent or even bankrupt. As illustrated week after week on the TV programme 'Dragons Den', most entrepreneurs do not understand the difference between gross margin and net profit.

In summary, people are your most important resource and they will gradually become experts in specialised fields of operation. If you can't manage this structure yourself then employ someone who can.

Products

It is obvious that without a product or service you cannot really have a company. However, we are in this book considering growth rather than forming a new company. This therefore puts products behind people in order of importance as you can obviously grow without new products but you will need more people to have growth.

Your product (or service) must bring real benefits to potential customers. It will have features and advantages that will need explaining but customers buy benefits and these must be very clearly identified.

It is virtually impossible to give advice about products as they are very particular to each company. You can meet price or technical competition and even geographic locality challenges. It pays you to be very aware of your competitors' products and the claims they make. Where possible, a programme of continuous improvements should be attempted even if you are protected by patent or copyright. New and better competitors may develop products that are better than yours without the need to infringe your intellectual property.

Money

If you think of money as the lubricant of your business engine then you can easily understand its importance to your company's growth. Without lubricant the engine will seize, making continuity impossible, let alone growth. The section on financial planning will help understand the use of this vital ingredient.

Premises

Many start-ups work from home but growth will need suitable premises. Initially early stage growth may take place in poor quality premises but moving to better ones will depend somewhat on where your workforce live and whether your customers need to visit you as is the case in retail operations.

With regard to location, once again I defer to Bill Hewlett and David Packard. They decided that where they needed new factories they would create them where people liked to live. This was easier in the US than in crowded England but the principle remains a good one. It is much easier to attract new high quality staff where the office or factory is in pleasant surroundings. It is interesting to note the approach of many new internet companies where they have turned the workplace into a fun location and made working time very flexible. The growth of internet and wireless-enabled technologies has opened up a very large range of attractive working practices. I personally do not like working alone and permanently remote from others, only communicating by some electronic device. I like and believe it important to meet with other people in my team in a face-to-face manner.

Your resources have to change

In the previous section I dealt primarily with the main assets used in a company and how to understand them. However, there is not only the nature and range of assets, there is the matter of how they interact with each other both in individual interactions and as groups. There is no simple, straightforward, universal approach. Each company will have its own unique range of resources and this will be multiplied by the differing cultures and management styles involved.

In this section I am basing it on an article originally written for the magazine *South East Business* in September 2000 and now updated. All increases in resources have some positive effects but also will have some negative aspects as well which have to be monitored carefully.

11. THE TWO TYPES OF CAPITAL

1. FIXED CAPITAL AND WORKING CAPITAL

Fixed Capital

Is just what it says.

Any money which is spent on assets for the company which is not recoverable quickly or without selling the asset. For example, production machinery or office equipment used in the running of the business.

Different types of companies will have differing needs for fixed capital investments. Manufacturing companies will usually have a greater need than trading companies and are therefore usually more difficult to start. To help this situation there are a wide variety of financial products available from banks or other financial institutions. The most obvious is Hire Purchase which can be used to finance the acquisition of fixed assets that have a resale value. This will include cars, computers, desks and chairs, etc. There are also leases and stock financing. These reduce the immediate pressure on financing fixed assets but of course the repayments continue into the future and will reduce your positive cash flow from sales activity.

In Limited Liability companies the shareholders usually provide the initial fixed investments either directly with cash or by guaranteeing any form of loan finance. As a company grows it is likely that it will need increasing amounts of capital investment. One hurdle that occurs with this situation is where production cannot be increased incrementally but has to take place in significant chunks. For example, if a product is made on automated machinery, that machinery will have a definite capacity. If you need to increase your production you have to buy a complete new automated machine which doubles your capacity. If you can only foresee a 40% growth then your production costs per item will increase and may not be competitive.

Fixed capital investments should be approached with cautious calculation. These difficulties explain why many companies choose to have their products made by outside contractors. It is the outside contractors who effectively make the investment in machinery but they can spread the cost over many customers. There are other reasons for subcontracting production to others but the reduction in need for capital investment is often a powerful one.

Working Capital

Differs from fixed capital in that it is used to finance the actual operation of the company and not its fixed capital infrastructure. It covers such things as the Manufacturing Overheads such as wages, electricity etc., and Sales Overheads such as wages, advertising, rent, etc. These are detailed elsewhere in this book, where these costs are discussed in detail.

The principal source for increasing working capital is your profits. This need is the primary reason to make a good profit on your sales. Without profits you cannot repay loans used for fixed capital investment. Further, you cannot take on more staff or increase wages, but most importantly of all you will not be able to finance your sales growth.

A good way to understand the importance of profits in growing a company is to consider the following calculations.

Firstly, calculate how many times in a year that you are able to turn over your working capital. This is the time from when you first start to use your money to make or buy products to the date that your customers' money is in your bank.

It is easiest to consider buying and reselling a product. If you choose to buy a product you can either take as the start date when you pay your customer, or a more cautious approach, using the date that you either place the order or when you get the invoice.

Take this date and when the money is in your bank, to calculate how long your money is tied up in this process. For my companies this was rarely less than 3 months and thus I could calculate my working capital over 4 times a year (supermarkets do this in a couple of days).

The profits you can use are your after-tax profit less any dividends paid to your shareholders and any capital investments you need.

If your pre-tax profits are 10% of sales of

£1million, say £100k, then with tax at 20% you will have £80k left. Dividends will perhaps be £30k, leaving £50k. Capital expenditure may be £20k, leaving £30k to finance increased trade. Turning over this £30k four times a year means that sales can increase by £120k or 12% per annum. I suggest you do these calculations by regularly changing the numbers to meet current reality.

This is part of the reason that internet companies are so valuable and can grow explosively. They have enormous margins and low production costs.

You can of course borrow money against your improved balance sheet but there are reasons to do this cautiously.

Increasing borrowing to finance growth must be approached with caution and a full understanding of the terms under which this borrowing takes place and in particular any assets that are used as security for the loan. There are loans such as factoring that use your invoices as security and stock financing loans which use your warehouse stock as collateral.

Always remember that loans have to be repaid and make certain you can do so when needed.

2. HOW TO VALUE YOUR COMPANY TO ATTRACT INVESTMENT

People may well want to invest in your venture. If you are a company or partnership you can offer to sell shares or a partnership. Such investments are often difficult to value and can turn out to cause conflict.

For example, if you sell shares you need to be able to value your company. The value is at the end of the day a *'best guess'*. A valuation will often tend to be a multiple of the average profits for the last 3 years. For example, if the average profits have been £50,000 and a multiple of 10 is decided on as reasonable, the value will be £500,000.

This has a variant known as EBITDA; this stands for **E**arnings **B**efore **I**nterest, **T**ax, **D**epreciation and **A**mortisations. Once again, a multiplier will be applied. EBITDA ratings are principally used by professional investors.

A common mistake in deciding on a value for a company is that the founder does not include their salary and costs into the P/L account in order to increase profits and thus value. This rarely succeeds. The reasons why an individual will want to buy into your company are many and varied. It may just be to hope for a future capital gain, or that it results in them gaining employment and a salary.

It is common to overvalue a company when valuing it for a share sale. This will often be compounded by being willing only to sell a small percentage of shares. A seller, to be successful, must take into account the investors' reasons in making the purchase. Further, the company's Memorandum and Articles will contain different rights to different levels of shareholding.

The most obvious split lies at the 50% mark. To own 50% and one share gains effective power over the company's activities. This simple example may have many other companions. Some examples are that if you own less than 10% you can be forced to sell. With quoted companies owning over 30% raises a liability to make an offer to buy out all the other shareholders. If you hold over 25% then you may be able to block motions made at a Board or General Meeting. When dealing with purchase of shares or a partnership it is vital to get good legal and financial advice. It will also repay you very well to read the 'Memorandums and Articles'.

3. FINANCIAL PLANNING

For myself, from the beginning, I decided to build a Limited Liability Company and at first had only 31% shareholding. I relied on another colleague with 20% to hold control against outside investors. In a negotiation detailed elsewhere I built my initial 31% to 61% by buying out an initial investor. Without this change in power I do not think we would have succeeded in floating the company, as the others would have been too greedy and uncertain.

So much for investment to raise working capital. The main alternative is to borrow it, and there are a large number of borrowing mechanisms. In almost every case the loan will be given but secured against the value of some or all of your tradable assets.

Examples of tradable assets are: your house (!!!), stock, premises, capital equipment, cars, debtors. Hang on to your house and only use it if you have no alternative. Banks like taking a charge over your house, as it often is a very tradable item. Beware though, they are very reluctant to release the charge when your crisis is solved.

I found that the financial power of invoice discounting or factoring provided the cash flow we needed when growing rapidly. They needed informed use, as if wrongly used they could result in very challenging circumstances. Most certainly they should not be used to fund losses.

We used factoring from a very early stage because the formula suited our processes very much indeed. A major part of our business was importing high-value goods from abroad and invoicing them to customers within 7 days of their despatch to us. We were allowed 30 days' credit by our suppliers but some of our major customers would take 60 or even 90 days to pay. If done from our own working capital we would have to finance one or even two months of purchase. We could not have survived very long at all. Our trading formula was relatively simple.

We purchased the goods and invoiced them to our customers marked up by 50%, giving a 33.3% gross margin.

We spent 20% of our revenues on overhead expenditure, leaving a notional pre-tax profit of 13%. The factoring company took control of our invoices and our customers were instructed to pay the factoring company.

When the Factors got our invoice they forwarded 80% of the invoice value to us within a few days. They paid us the remaining 20% when they were paid by the customer.

Our original costs represented 66.6% of our sales price, so that the 80% advance allowed us to pay the supplier on time and still have an overhead contribution of 13.4% which covered all the major overheads such as salaries and rent. For many overheads we had up to 60 days' credit, once again easing cash flow. There was obviously a charge by the Factors but it was low in comparison to the increased sales we could achieve. All in all we found this system worked well for us but we always supervised it carefully so as not to fool ourselves about our cash situation.

4. CREDIT RATINGS

Good ones are vital.

As we always, but always paid our Japanese suppliers on time, we were rated as very credit-worthy by the Japanese government trade association MITI.

We could only use Factoring in the UK so sales to the USA were not covered. However, because of our credit rating and our exporting to the USA, our Japanese bank (Dai Ichi Kangyo) was prepared to finance these by using Promissory Notes. Essentially these are promises to pay an invoice at a given time in the future, hence '*Promissory Note*'.

I asked the bank manager in Tokyo how much credit we could have and his reply put English banks to shame. He said that as were credit-worthy and selling Japanese exports to credit-worthy customers in the USA, there was no limit.

Overall Japan's banks allowed us over 12 times the finance available than from the UK banks. They were very trade oriented rather than asset fixated.

There are a very wide range of specialised financial arrangements available from British banks, ranging from Hire Purchase to Stock Financing. My suggestion is that you spend a lot of time uncovering these arrangements and study them carefully until you understand them in minute detail. They will mostly be asset based but try to exclude your home.

5. LOANS

Never forget that all loans have to be repaid and require interest payments. Overdrafts are a very convenient and flexible way to finance cash flow as long as you stay within the agreed limits, you can use it in varying amounts and only pay interest on the actual amount in use. The main problem with overdrafts is that they can be recalled (cancelled) at any time the bank feels they may be at risk.

As an alternative you can consider a term loan. This is just what it says. The bank lends you an agreed sum of money, say £100k, to be repaid with interest over 10 years. The great advantage of this is that provided you keep up the payments then the money is always available. The disadvantage is that it is not flexible; if you need more it will require a new loan. More on these subjects is covered in the finance section of this book.

The upside of increasing working capital is that it makes it possible to grow your business. The negative aspects are that also can increase your obligations and risks. As examples, you may need to pay shareholders some dividends. You may need to pay interest, thus reducing your profit margin, and finally it may need you to put your assets at risk by using them as security.

6. INCREASE OR DECREASE SUPPLIERS

I put both increase and decrease of suppliers because each can be both a benefit and a hazard depending on the stage of your business.

When you start out it is most likely that you will only have a very limited range of suppliers (maybe only one) as you haven't enough business to get the attention of any others. The next stage is often a move to have at least two suppliers for each item so that if one fails the other can keep you going. Further, of course, it creates the opportunity for some competition.

In Densitron, when acting as a supplier we worked hard wherever possible to be a sole supplier. To do this we concentrated on having our own brand of superior products with unique features. We worked closely and very helpfully with the design section of a company to get our products incorporated at an early stage of development. When it came to the buyers department we aimed to be the only solution available for them to buy. We didn't misuse this situation by charging exorbitant prices so that we didn't alienate the whole company. By delivering both outstanding products and service we gained the trust of the company and avoided a damaging price war.

7. SOLE SUPPLIER

The final stage of this progression is where a very big company will aim to deal with only one supplier for a particular product. This was pioneered by the Japanese car industry and is the reason they created such a reputation for quality.

For each component they sought to be in control of the whole supply chain, right back to the mining of the iron or other basic material. Using steel as an example, Quality Control was under the car company's control, from choosing what mine to source to the creation of the steel used in the body work and its final painting. They did this for all components including engines and electronics. The suppliers were rewarded by constant high-quantity orders, but they yielded their independence and became dominated by the car giants who ultimately decided what profits they made. They were allowed to exist but not determine their lifestyle.

8. AN EXAMPLE OF JAPANESE COMPETITION

A particular example from my own past concerns our introduction to such a situation in the manufacture of high-quality, advanced technology flashbulbs. These were used on the outside of aircraft or other high-reliability situations. We had inherited this capability when we bought a small microwave company (Nore Microwave) from a car bulb manufacturer. They had no plans for it and we got it for nothing. It was predominately a small-volume, hand-built product. Our sales were about 2,000 a year but they were very highly priced, so made a good contribution.

At that time in another part of the company we sold miniature filament lamps imported from Japan. Once, when visiting the manufacturer, we discussed a problem they had. One of their customers, a very large manufacturer of machinery, was planning to introduce a much faster automated ticket machine for the surface and underground railways. Due to the wide variety of tickets to be issued they were to be printed at the moment of purchase.

To do this they had a fast-drying ink which was set by an intense flash of light (a flashbulb!). The problem our partner had was they had no idea how to make flashbulbs. Thinking that it would be a small-volume item like in England, I offered to let them visit our factory and learn how to make flashbulbs. They came in a team and listened to everything we said and photographed everything we did; they then went back to Japan.

About six months later I again visited the company and asked how they were progressing with production of the flashbulbs. The MD said they were going well but had *only* got production up to 5,000 pieces PER MONTH! This against our level after many years of 2,000 per YEAR. I immediately asked to see the production line. What a shock. There was a fully operational automated production line. I asked how they had done this.

The answer was that they were sole lamp supplier to the large Japanese company (maybe Mitsubishi from memory). The customer was to be the sole supplier of automated ticket machines to all the railways and thus the need for high volume. Mitsubishi had told our supplier to make flashbulbs. The volumes required demanded a fully automated production process. The bulb maker, who already made high volume filament lamps on automated production lines, designed new ones for the flashbulbs. Mitsubishi manufacturing went to their sister company Mitsubishi Bank and told them to supply all the money needed to make the production lines and finance the production itself.

It was all done in 6 months due to the money needs being met by the bank. This all happened in the 1970s.

How could we in Britain compete with this powerhouse and very logical process? I doubt whether I had been able to get to discuss the matter with a bank manager within this time scale. I certainly would not have been able to borrow the money to carry out the building work without assets to borrow against. The Japanese all worked together to a common end and I imported the results into the USA and Europe – our know-how, their market, and money. One interesting fact is of course that we probably made more money in the trading sales worldwide than they did in the manufacturing process.

The arrival of the Japanese car industry into the UK has brought us a lot of benefits, but I wonder where the most profit is made and where the most employment is (a very important point in recent times with much cross-border migration seeking employment and money).

I hope these stories help illustrate some of the complexities in building and growing a company.

12. FORECASTING SALES AND FINANCIAL PLANNING

I hold that financial planning is the most vital part in running a growing company, particularly with regard to cash flow. However, in a growing business it is clear that the future will not be the same as the present. Therefore you must make effective financial future plans based upon a range of forecasts. The most important of these is the forward sales forecast. In that it is impossible to know the actual future, it is important to develop a range of techniques and procedures to make forecasting as useful as possible.

The simplest forecast is to draw a graph of monthly sales and then draw a line through the recent past (up to, say, three years) and extend it forward at the same slope.

There are some obvious difficulties with this approach. The first is that past sales may not be either on a straight line or a smooth curve. There are a variety of techniques available to help you overcome this problem.

The first of these is to use techniques that reduce the amount of variability that exist in monthly sales figures.

This is called SMOOTHING and once again there are various methodologies. I recommend one that I found most useful which is called a *moving monthly average*. Essentially you start your graph at the end of the first quarter of sales you intend to use as base data. Let us assume your year starts on January 1st. Add together January, February, and March sales figures and divide by three, and plot this number as your March sales figure. It is obviously enough an average of the first quarter's sales. It is what follows that makes it more useful. You move forward on your graph, plotting each month as the average of the previous three months' sales. This will smooth out to a large amount the variability between monthly sales. This smoother graph will be easier to project forward either as a straight line or a curve. In forward forecasting a curve you can either use a computer program or simply just use your eyes.

Having done what is called 'a moving monthly average' (MMA), you can also use the same technique either over a six-month period or even a yearly one (MYA) if you have enough data. I found that using a combination of both an MMA and an MYA helped produce more accurate forecasting, as the MMA helped smooth the sales figures and the MYA gave a better indication of long-term trends.

1. SAFER FORECASTING

It is important to avoid any over-enthusiastic forward projections as these will distort your financial needs.

I always felt that it is vital to have alternative plans. I would take the 'projected forward forecast' and then put two alternative graphs along it. One would be the maximum performance I could envisage and the other the slowest growth likely to happen.

In this way I could have a main plan but already have alternatives if it didn't happen. I hold it is too late to start creating a plan when difficulties occur. Together with the alternative plans, we used a discipline protocol to trigger our change between plans. We monitored the accuracy of our performance against plan on a monthly basis. If our performance differed from the plan by a set amount in a month it was noted. If the second month differed by a similar amount in the same direction, then a decision would be made on what alternative should be considered for use. If the third month followed the same amount and direction of change, the pre-prepared plan was implemented. Using these techniques or similar ones reduced the danger of incorrect sales forecasting.

Sales forces routinely create optimistic sales forecasts which can cause wasted increased resources, whilst accountants tend to be more pessimistic, which can cause a lack of resources and lost opportunities. Using a variable forecasting method will reduce the risk of suffering either of these outcomes.

2. USING SALES FORECAST IN FINANCIAL FORECASTING

Having created a sales forecast, then a range of financial forecasts can be prepared using similar techniques. The most important, because it is short term and fast changing, is the *Cash Flow Forecast*. The slowest moving but still vital is the capital requirements to support the Balance Sheet.

This has been covered in the preceding section on the main resources of Products, Premises, People, and Money.

With all this data, financial plans can be made for all the essential parts of the business. You should use the services of a trained accountant to help make these plans. A Management Accountant may well be the best option in forward planning, although Chartered Accountants may be just as appropriate.

A good guide to the range of financial plans is had by using the two main company financial reports as a guide. These are the Profit and Loss account for the fine detail of costs and overheads, with the Balance Sheet giving guidance for capital needs.

Of particular importance is using the P&L report to control the percentages of costs for each main category. The range of these costs is largely determined by whether you are manufacturing, trading, or selling time.

In manufacturing you will have the basic costs of making the items. These may include factory costs, raw materials, machinery and depreciation, manufacturing, employees and transport. It is normal to add all these up and develop a basic 'in-warehouse cost' for the product. This is sometimes referred to as the 'prime cost'.

If you are trading by buying ready-made products then you should create the same known, 'in-warehouse costs'. Sometimes the 'in-warehouse cost' is made the same as the purchase price, but it is probably better to add any costs such as transport, import duty, and even a charge for warehousing rental. This represents the true value (or cost) of the stock in your warehouse. This value of course is only released when the goods are sold AND paid for. Stock and debtors represent dead capital which prevents its use in newer stock or sales. This is why major retailers have regular discount sales to release the capital locked up in slow moving stock.

In summary, I am advising using a variety of techniques to forecast the three best possible guesses for future sales. These are: the fastest growth that is likely, the slowest that can be tolerated, and one between these that can be regarded as an ideal outcome.

You then use these sales forecasts to develop a range of financial plans which cover both your quickly varying cash flow requirements and the longer-term capital requirements. Both of these are important but it is often the cash flow errors that can be fatal to a company's future. As advised, running out of cash (insolvency) is a main cause of fast-growing profitable companies failing. All the money will be tied up in stock and debtors resulting in creditors (often your bank) taking you to court. Profit is only real when it is in *your bank*.

13. TAX ISSUES

It is very, very important to understand your tax liabilities. There is:

1) **Corporation Tax**: Paid on your profits at varying rates depending on your level of profit.

2) **VAT (Value Added Tax)**: Paid on all relevant commercial transactions.

3) **National Insurance**: Paid to the government on behalf of your employees for the NHS.

4) **PAYE (Pay As You Earn)**: A proportion of each employee's personal tax.

5) **Stamp Duty:** Paid on property or land transactions.

6) **Import Duty:** Paid on some imports at varying rates.

7) **Excise Duty:** Paid on alcohol.

Personally I found tax issues to be the most complex of all the challenges in a growing business. Taxation is of itself complex and detailed, but also changed by governments whenever the urge takes them, to get more income. I most strongly urge you to get first-class tax advice.

There are not only a multiplicity of taxes, there are

also a variety of offsets and reliefs.

Whatever you do, don't try to outwit the tax system, and most importantly do not undertake any illegal activities. The penalties are severe. It may be that you make mistakes in a report. If you do this and find it before the taxman, let them know as soon as possible and have some idea of how you will rectify the error.

Apparently it was once said and very often repeated, *'There are only two certainties in life. They are Taxation and Death'*. Very true.

14. WHAT GETS IN THE WAY OF GROWTH?

There are probably an untold number of barriers to growth but I am putting forward the following as issues you may not otherwise consider fully.

1. COMPETITION

Never underestimate your competitors. If they haven't been very active this can change if they see you growing. They may have plans that they haven't publicised. They may take over another business. They may take on new designers or a new Sales Director. These are unknown unknowns and you should be wary of them, and have plans to deal with any potential challenges.

Patenting or copyrighting can help. With regard to personnel changes you can monitor job adverts to keep an eye on your competitors. One thing I used to do was to advertise highly paid jobs for salesmen or design engineers. This would usually result in some of our competitors' staff applying for these jobs, which in reality did not exist. The senior management of the competitors would worry about what we were up to as there was usually a hint of technical breakthroughs.

The staff we interviewed would with careful questioning reveal what the competitors were doing in their departments. If we did find a very talented individual we would actually make an offer and create a proper job for them. Not entirely gentlemanly, but very competitive. If you are going to grow, it may well be that you take some of the increased business from competitors and they will react; so get your retaliation in first.

2. OPTIMISM

One rarely considered barrier to growth is 'over-optimism'. It is very good to have a high level of optimism but it should be allied to a level of scepticism, but no cynicism. This is not an easy balance to achieve. I certainly erred on the side of over-optimism and sometimes paid dearly for it.

The big objective for a sceptical attitude is to recognise when your plans are in reality wrong. Ploughing on with a project that is not reaching its objectives is mostly wrong. At the very least a review of the objectives should take place and the plans modified where possible.

I regularly watch the TV show Dragons Den. It seems from that show that a large number of applicants have hopelessly over-optimistic views of their business proposition. This is especially true of the valuations they apply to their companies. They seem to forget that the Dragons only invest to get a financial return in that investment. What happens on that show replicates my experiences when offering advice to other companies.

I think it is fair to say that a large number, if not a majority of smaller companies would like to grow, but only on the condition that it remains basically the same company. Growth requires the management to change its methodology particularly with regard to the company's internal communication systems. Growth requires constant change in personnel and operational structures. Just hoping that it can be run the same as in the past rarely works. I found attending various business schools and paying attention to other companies that I visited helped me cope with what at times were major changes in the company's operations.

The biggest change of course was when we became a public company. We were subject to close scrutiny and detailed informed questioning. The interrogators were experienced investors who had the benefit of meeting large numbers of differing companies and their Directors. I found I could learn much from the questions they asked.

Another source of help was through our non-executive directors, who brought a differing range of experiences to the table. The professions of accountants and lawyers could also be a source of good information to the inquiring mind. They could help by indicating how other companies had overcome specific problems.

By far the most important component is, however, the willingness of the directors and managers to be open-minded and willing to learn and change. Curiosity allied to intelligence is needed to underpin the changes demanded by growth.

3. FEAR OF CHANGE

This challenge is currently almost endemic in the whole of British society. These days any proposed change in our built environment is met with vociferous opposition. High-speed railways; no way! New runways; forget it! Build more houses; not in my locality! Change our working methods; all out! All of this from the nation that brought the Industrial Revolution to the world. We created the Magna Carta. We created the world's first parliamentary democracy. We went into the world and built the biggest ever trading empire.

As the guiding impulse behind your company's growth plans you must be aware of the doomsters and rebut them as soon as they put their heads over the parapet. I found that although being one myself, that engineers had a reflex reply to any new approach. Having listened to the explanation their first response tended to be, "The problem with that idea is…"

My method to deal with this was to impose a *fine* on the first person to say this phrase. The money from the fine was used to help fund the company's Christmas party. The way to avoid the fine was to propose a change in the proposition that would help avoid a specific difficulty. Innovative new ideas earned credit whilst negative criticism attracted punishment. It worked.

I have a theory as to why people will tend to forecast negative outcomes. It is that this approach is of low risk to one's status in the group.

If the outcome is as bad as you have predicted you

get immediate kudos by exclaiming, "I told you so," sometimes followed by, "but you wouldn't listen." Your status as a wise head is reinforced.

What if you are wrong and the outcome is magnificent? Nobody cares because they are so happy. If someone remarks on your forecast you just smile and say, "I was just ensuring we looked at the project from all sides and thus indeed avoided the problem."

Being a Doomster is a safe option. Forging ahead with new ideas is always a risk. However, the best rewards come from taking informed risks.

4. POOR OR DISORGANISED MANAGEMENT

The opportunity to grow can and will occur in a sporadic manner. Even what appears to be a well-planned period of growth probably started by a chance happening. This at least was my experience. I found that new opportunities constantly occurred. Many of them were ultimately not able to sustain early promise but those that did required constant change in the company's plans and the approach taken by the management.

I suspect that most companies start out like I did, with a new approach to an existing market. I have elsewhere given some details of how Densitron started and grew. One characteristic I have is the willingness to explore new ideas but in doing so base my actions on past experiences and knowledge. Further, I am always willing to change my plans if better opportunities arise.

I think the most extreme example came early on in Densitron's activities.

My original new approach was based upon selling electronic components to what was known as the professional electronics industry (e.g. Defence and Scientific) rather than the one based upon domestic devices such as televisions and radios.

Many of these 'professional' components were sold through stocking distributors. The salespeople from these distributors were by and large not of high technical calibre and sold primarily on a price and delivery basis. The best situation was where the distributor had it in stock with the lowest price. This was an almost unbeatable proposition. The problem occurred when there was no existing component that could solve a particular design challenge.

The salesman could not understand the technical issues involved and consequently the component manufacturer never got any meaningful feedback. Being a widely experienced design engineer turned salesman, I could often understand the problem and propose a solution based upon some rather small changes to an existing product.

I would not sell under a supplier's brand but negotiated with them to make the changes needed for a sale. I would buy from them under what was called the 'white box trade'. The product was sold to me without the manufacturer's name either on the component or the box it was packed in. It would be sold under my brand name.

This was the core idea, although I did also sell some marked components on an exclusive basis. I avoided a price and delivery approach like the plague. The main reason for this was that a stocking distributor needed large amounts of capital for stock (which I lacked) and was also boring.

5. BANKS

Banks get a lot of blame for not financing small companies more fully.

I hold that the role of banks is misunderstood by all politicians and most start-up and small, growing companies. I include myself in this statement when in the early stages of Densitron's growth, I was lucky in choosing my first investing partners, two senior executives at Hewlett Packard UK. We first approached their bank, the Bank of Scotland, to ask for financing for the various projects. The management of the Bank of Scotland in Edinburgh were worried that if they didn't support us it might damage their relationship with HP. As a consequence they supported our ambitions more liberally than if I had approached them myself.

We didn't realise this situation until many years later, by which time we had become a good customer to them.

The point about the main High Street banks is that in lending to you they are in fact lending you other people's money which has been deposited with them for safe keeping and interest income. They expect only to lend against liquid disposable assets in case you should default on a loan. The idea they lend against your dreams and aspirations is wrong. You need a strong and well-structured Balance Sheet. You need a cash flow that can pay interest charges and profits that will enable you to repay the loan if necessary. It is very probable that you will need a share capital input as well as a bank loan.

Remember, banks have a wide range of other financial products to help finance your business. I have touched upon these in the section dealing with Working Capital.

Banks are vital to a strong economy but they differ radically from investors. There are Merchant Banks and Investment Banks, but these are primarily aimed at larger companies.

These day CROWDFUNDING activities can offer some of the features of a flexible bank. These are based upon active lenders splitting up a specific loan into manageable sections with the calculated risk determining the interest charged. This innovation is transforming the loan market for smaller growing companies.

A final note is that if you are importing or exporting, the exchange rate between various currencies can have a major effect on your trade and expected profitability. You can secure positions by purchasing your foreign currency ahead of your actual usage to ensure you can make the profits you expect. You can even take options on the future values of currencies you intend to use. Almost all banks will have capability in this area.

6. THE GOVERNMENT

The government can have enormous impact upon a company's fortunes. It can change any or all of the tax regimes detailed earlier in the book. Just consider the situation that the Greek Government has got into, with banks having to control how much money they will issue and even make them close. They have even closed the Stock Exchange.

Our own government in my time imposed a three-day week, and raised the VAT from around 10% to 25%, causing real cash flow problems. They have altered personal and corporation tax regularly. It pays to pay close attention to government actions. As we are here considering the well-established growing business it is probable you will have your own financial and even legal advisers. It is prudent to ask them for advice about government decisions.

Be wary of government actions. Politicians tend not to be long-term thinkers.

15. YOUR ABILITIES MUST BE SUITABLE

The most important component in this quest for growth is the person/people who is/are to create the plans and carry them out. I have written most of this book in the singular so that it is suitable for an individual entrepreneur to read and get ideas from its content. However, I believe that the majority of effective growth is achieved by teams of people.

For the individual entrepreneur I strongly recommend using one of the personality or aptitude tests that are available free on the internet. These will help you understand your capabilities more fully. There is a danger that an individual entering a period of growth will take on too much and become overworked. This in turn can lead to mental exhaustion and ill health.

In the case where growth is occurring after the successful creation of a new venture it is probable that the founder will have attracted some employees and at least one other manager to confer with.

PERSONALITY TRAITS NEEDED FOR GROWTH.

1. PROJECTING AMBITIONS FOR ALL STAFF

This may seem obvious but it is rarely done well. In an earlier part of this book I dealt with avoiding spin, which is where basically weak ideas are introduced as game changers. Staff will always recognise spin and if used by managers will cause their reputation to diminish.

What is presented as a major step forward by the company is interpreted by staff as a move by the managers to get more status, power, and salary. They are probably not far wrong.

Being ambitious for all staff is a continuous process, not an occasional event. Staff must feel valued and respected. They should get regular contact with knowledgeable senior staff. They should receive regular training and of course get satisfactory pay levels and opportunity for promotion.

If all this is taken care of, then when an exciting advance for the company is announced, they will be inclined to believe it and most importantly enthusiastically support it.

The public announcements by Apple are examples of outstanding ambition well and excitingly presented. Their customers and staff believe them because they do what they say they will do.

2. BE ARTICULATE AND BELIEVABLE

If you are to grow your business you will have to interface not only with your staff but with banks, solicitors, accountants and maybe the media.

If you are not naturally articulate then take some training. It cannot change you into Steve Jobs but it can help. If you cannot do public announcements then share them with someone who can. If you are the boss, don't hide yourself away. You must do the basic announcement yourself and then introduce someone to explain the details. This way you can be seen to be in charge but with supporters.

Early on in my career when working for Westinghouse Brake and Signal Company as head of product development, I worked for a very capable but inarticulate chief engineer. He had to report regularly to the Board of Directors on our engineering progress. They became very frustrated with him as he struggled to explain our various engineering ventures. Eventually he decided to take me with him into Board meetings to do the technical explanations in ways they could understand. Unfortunately he never explained my more junior role as head of R&D. In time, the Board, in their ignorance decided that I knew our business better than my boss and sacked him.

In turn they offered me the job of Chief Engineer on a six-month trial basis. If it didn't work out I would be sacked in my turn. It was a take it or leave it offer so I took it and luckily did the job well enough to retain the post, which became very adventurous as my entrepreneurial tendencies kicked in. My predecessor was the better engineer but I could communicate to and enthuse others where he couldn't.

3. BIG LESSONS - TRUST OTHERS CAREFULLY

If you are going to grow your business by any significant amount you will at various stages have to trust others. This applies to staff you employ and to outsiders. You can put in some safeguards for your own staff but outsiders are more difficult. You can choose to use lawyers but this will be very expensive. You can learn to control risks but you will have, at times, to trust others.

One technique I used for myself in calculating a risk was to work out the main outcomes that would ensue if my trust was not well placed.

The conversation with myself was something like a sequence of questions I posed to myself.

For example: Will I die? Will I go bankrupt? How much can I lose? Can I afford this? Etc., etc. I imagined the worst of outcomes and if I felt that I could survive the worst and the upside was worthwhile I would go ahead and trust (with limits) the person or situation. At the same time I would have developed a plan of action for dealing with the worst case. Over a 60-year working life I prospered, sometimes with heartache but overall it all worked out to my advantage.

4. TRUST YOURSELF

It may seem obvious that you have to trust

yourself. This can be a learned technique or an innate characteristic. My personality profile identifies my main attitude to risk is this – I always assume that anything, venture or action, will go wrong. I also assume that I can put it right. By and large this turned out to be true. Learning to trust yourself is helped by using the techniques outlined above. Always go into a venture with a plan of how to deal with failure. Sometimes this still goes wrong but here you will have to learn how to pick yourself up and start again (or not).

5. DO WHAT YOU SAY YOU WILL DO

If something does go seriously wrong and you really cannot honour your word, then negotiate a new arrangement, don't just walk away. A reputation for honesty and good practice is invaluable.

6. MANAGEMENT TEAMS

I strongly recommend that a management team is created and in the case of a Ltd company a proper Board of Directors. In both cases these groups of either managers or directors should be considered as a team. To help with this process I found that the books and tests created by Professor Belbin (available online) are a most excellent help in understanding the various roles played in successful teams. He discovered that teams should have within them a total of only 9 roles. In order to limit the number of actual people on the team it is necessary that some individual play two or more roles. However, all of this is explained fully in his writings and anything I say here will be a pale shadow of the real thing.

My contribution is to encourage the creation of management and director's teams. In my various consulting roles I found the most regular cause of underperformance was down to an inadequate Board of Directors. They in turn appointed an inadequate management structure. As a company grows it will need to change its management regularly and its directors only slightly less frequently.

I was very fortunate in that I started out with 3 high-quality investors plus myself, who all had experience of director-level activities. As a consequence, whenever we met it was by default a directors' meeting for which we took notes. I was the only Executive Director, with the others all being non-executive. We had me in the role of MD and Sales Director. We had another who was a chartered accountant as Finance Director. The MD of HP became Chairman and the last one was the only one to have started and owned an actual company. He acted in the role of Monitor Evaluator (a Belbin category).

It came as a shock to me to realise that very few start-ups of mid-sized family companies bothered to have a proper Board of Directors. Even more surprising was the failure to appoint a properly qualified accountant into the board/management teams. In fact, the differing roles of managers and directors was a very blurred subject. I repeat, I think time spent on understanding these issues and how they relate to growth is rarely, if ever, wasted.

After this short digression into the roles of teams in growth I return to the individual who should lead this growth project. They should project and enthuse about ambition. They should be able to lead and motivate others, not by dictating but rather by example and motivation. They should manage by objectives, be articulate and believable. The setting of unrealistic targets is a very common mistake.

Plans should set achievable targets so the belief and enthusiasm grows over time. Nothing is more depressing than constantly setting targets which do not get met. There is nothing wrong with setting achievable targets and then indicating a higher performance as an ambition.

Thus you can have in ascending order of difficulty: a **Forecast,** a **Target,** an **Aim,** or **Ambition.**

Be realistic and encourage.

Learn to trust others and eliminate those you can't trust.

TRUST YOURSELF.

DO WHAT YOU SAY YOU WILL DO.

RECOGNISE YOUR LIMITS AND TAKE ADVICE.

ADDENDUM 1

'CLIFF CLARIFIES BUSINESS GROWTH'

THE MAIN CONTENTS OF THIS ADDENDUM GIVE A RANGE OF IDEAS COVERING SOME MANAGEMENT RULES AND BEST PRACTICE FOR A GROWING COMPANY.

THESE GUIDELINE RULES ARE TAKEN FROM MY OWN PERSONAL EXPERIENCES BOTH WITHIN MY OWN COMPANY AND WORKING FOR OTHERS.

THEY MAY NOT SUIT YOUR OWN ENTERPRISE BUT SHOULD ENCOURAGE YOU TO THINK ABOUT THE ISSUES HIGHLIGHTED.

WITHIN MY OWN COMPANY THEY WERE GATHERED TOGETHER IN A FOLDER AND ISSUED TO ALL MANAGERS.

FAILURE TO FOLLOW THEM INCURRED REAL PENALTIES.

I hope you find the notes helpful in growing your business safely.

CLIFF HARDCASTLE, OBE FIET

1. INDEX TO ADDENDUM

- WEEKLY REPORTS
- MONTHLY REPORTS

AUTHORISATION LEVELS

- ORDERS ON SUPPLIERS
- QUOTES AND CUSTOMER ORDERS
- CREDIT NOTES

SIGNATORY LEVELS

- APPROVALS BY ANY DIRECTOR
- APPROVAL BY MANAGING DIRECTOR NEEDED

OVERHEAD COSTS

- BOUGHT OUT OVERHEAD ITEMS
- NEW STAFF AND SALARIES
- CAPITAL EXPENDITURE
- FINANCIAL ISSUES
- SEALING OFFICIAL DOCUMENTS

STAFF COMPETENCIES

- GENERAL
- PRODUCT MANAGERS
- SALES MANAGERS
- MANAGING DIRECTOR
- RECRUITMENT POLICIES
- MAIN BOARD GUIDANCE

GUIDANCE FOR TRADING COMPANIES

- BEST PRACTICE
- GUIDANCE ON OVERHEAD IDEAL RATIOS
- CONTRACTUAL SALES TERMS AND CONDITIONS
- SCHEDULED ORDERS

GUIDANCE FOR MANUFACTURING COMPANIES

- GROSS MARGIN
- STOCKS
- SALES AND DEBTORS
- CASH FLOW
- DESIGN AND DEVELOPMENT
- CAPITAL EXPENDITURE

- GENERAL COMMENTS
- GUIDANCE ON OVERHEAD RATIOS

SUGGESTED SALES ACTIVITIES

- CURRENT PRODUCTS
- FUTURE PRODUCTS
- SALES STAFF
- SALES MANAGEMENT
- ADVERTISING, PR AND EXHIBITIONS
- LARGER ENQUIRIES

FINANCIAL ISSUES

- TREASURY POLICIES
- CURRENCY EXPOSURE POLICIES
- STAFF PROCEDURES FOR CURRENCY EXPOSURE
- BALANCE SHEET EXPOSURE
- MANAGING BALANCE SHEET ISSUES
- PROFIT AND LOSS EXPOSURE
- TRANSACTIONAL EXPOSURE
- CONTROLLING FINANCIAL RISKS
- BORROWING GENERAL GUIDANCE
- OVERSEAS BORROWINGS

CURRENCY EXPOSURE

- IDENTIFYING RISKS
- ASSESSING RISKS
- UNACCEPTABLE RISKS
- RISK LIMITATION
- BALANCE SHEET RISKS
- LONG TERM RISKS
- CREDIT RISKS

2. REPORTING PROCEDURES TO BE USED

1. Weekly Reports from Subsidiaries

When?

At close of business, Monday (if not available, by open of business on Tuesday). Major subsidiaries to report.

a) **Shipments** for past week, by major class of business (e.g. UK, Europe, USA and Asia);

   Forecast for next week, by major class of business;

   Forecast for rest of month.

Weekly 'Flash' report, Orders/Sales/Cash for each subsidiary.

b) **Cash Flow**

   Details of cash movement for past week;

   Variances vs previous week's forecast;

   Forecast for next 4 weeks;

   Reasons for any changes.

2. Monthly Cash and Earnings Forecast

a) **Forecast of:**

Sales

Purchases

Stock Movement

Gross Margin

b) **Cash Flow Forecast for 3 months, by week**

Together with explanations of changes from:

i) Previous forecast;

ii) For month 6 (i.e. first forecast) – budget

Timing: At end of calendar month at Head Office this will be consolidated, resulting in Group Cash and Earnings Forecasts, circulated to the Board.

3. Stock

On a monthly basis – Stock Reports required from as soon as available (say 1 week after month end) review Aged Debtors List.

3. SUMMARY OF AUTHORISATION LEVELS

Orders placed on Suppliers

Goods to be purchased for resale:

- Against orders received from customer – **Company Director**

- Additional parts against order received from customer/part top-up stock (to take advantage of supplier price band) – **Company Director**.

- Purely for stock – **Company Managing Director** if stock value level increases as a result.

All the above to be against an Official Purchase Order from a customer, i.e. signed by person authorised to do so for the value of the order.

Authority to Issue Quotations or to Accept Orders

- For standard products at standard prices – authorised by **Sales Engineer up to £5,000.** In excess of £5,000 to be **countersigned by Company Director**.

- For special products at standard prices – authorised by **Company Managing Director.**

- For products at special prices (i.e. below normal margin) – authorised by **Company Managing Director**.

- Standard contractual terms always apply. Exceptions to be approved by **CEO only.**

Credit Notes

- Where money is lost, to be authorised by main Board Director. Where invoice value is incorrect or goods faulty, by **Company Director**. Monthly lists to be issued. Debit Notes from customers are not accepted. Lists of cancelled orders should also be maintained.

Returned goods from customers: goods must not be accepted back into stores *without authorised number* obtainable from Managing Director.

4. DIRECTOR LEVEL SIGNATORY POWERS

Director approval needed:

- For a quotation with *Standard Terms and Conditions:*

- **Up to £100k or the equivalent in other currencies.**

- For a quotation with *Special Terms* i.e. non-standard margin, extended payment terms, buffer stock required etc., these *must* be discussed with the Managing Director and signed by that director.

There will be NO variation to the above.

Managing Director Approvals

- A quotation for budgetary purposes **£500k** or equivalent in other currencies.

- A quotation with *Standard Terms and Conditions*

- **£200k or the equivalent in other currencies.**

  For non-standard quotations **£100k** as sole signatory above this level, it must be discussed with another director and countersigned by that director.

Authority to Draw Goods from Stores

- Where credit limit terms are exceeded for

shipment to customer against computer-produced despatch documents, despatch documents must be authorised by **Company Director**.

- For issue against stock requisition – signed by **Company Director** for goods to the value of £5,000, indicating purpose for which goods have been requisitioned. For goods in excess of this value, requisition to be countersigned by **Finance Director**.

Design and Development Expenditure

Work in the Design and Development Department should be done against one or other of the following authorisations:

- Cost of sales work against order received from Group or outside company correctly authorised.

- Against specific Development Number.

Any new development should be the subject of a special application to incur expense against a new project, indicating the work involved and the detailed estimated costs. Such application is to be approved by **CEO.**

Provided the above authorities are in place, the orders for D&D supplies can be placed against the appropriate D&D Project Numbers, in same way as B/L purchases.

5. OVERHEAD COSTS

Bought-Out Overhead Items:

- To be supported by formal order to be signed by **Company Director** to £3,000 countersigned by any other Company Director for amounts in excess of £3,000.

- Property maintenance, staff advertising and staff welfare, other than private hospital accounts – orders up to £5,000 – **Human Resources**.

- Private hospital accounts to be approved by **CEO.**

- Mandatory costs, e.g. rates – invoices up to £5,000 to be signed by **Company Managing Director** and/or **Finance Director.** Over £5,000 countersigned by another Company Director.

- Periodic bills, e.g. light, heat, telephone etc. – signed by **Company Director.**

- Staff claims for the reimbursement of **expenses** – approved by respective **Company Director.**

- **Motor vehicle repairs** – all to be approved by **Fleet Manager** before expense incurred, where practical.

- **Travel** – in accordance with Group instructions, all international travel plans to be approved by **CEO**. Invoices subsequently to be cleared by individual who travelled and countersigned by Company Director.

- Insurance, legal, professional and audit – charges from outside sources to be cleared by **Finance Director** and countersigned by **Company Director.** Inter-company charges under these headings to be approved by Company Director.

- Taxis, courier – to be ordered by **secretary** using duplicate books held at Reception, to be sent to Accounts Department to be agreed to invoice when received. In-house transport to be used for preference when available.

Salaries and Appointment

- Vacancy to be approved by **Human Resources** prior to advertising (advertising to be placed through senior secretaries and senior manager.)

- All new appointments to be approved by the **CEO** before offer letter is despatched.

- All employment of temporary staff to be approved by **Human Resources.**

- If salary increases are within budget and forecast is being met, then approval of **Managing Director** is sufficient.

- Overtime – to be approved by the **Company Managing Director.**

- Payroll authorisation: Monthly control approved by **Finance Director**/and in his absence by another board Director.

Capital Expenditure

- Capital Expenditure budgets to be approved by main Board at the time of annual budget submission.

- Expenditure can only take place if *all* the elements of annual budget are being met or exceeded.

- Any variation of timing or value to be approved by the main Board.

- Design and Development is a capital expenditure and must be accounted for on a monthly basis.

- Motor vehicles – to be ordered against requisition drawn up by **Fleet/Transport Manager**, giving reasons for proposed purchase, and approved by **Finance Director/Director.**

- Capital expenditure of service nature, e.g. office equipment – up to £1,000 approved by **Company Managing Director,** or **Human Resources** provided such item has been included in capital budget. Items not in capital budget and all items over £1,000 to be approved by a **Board Director.**

- Any individual item of Capital Expenditure in excess of £10,000 to be approved by **CEO/Finance Director** and confirmed by **Board Director.**

Finance

- Cheque signing – Bank Mandates in accordance with attached Schedule.

- Petty Cash – to be approved initially by a

175

Company Managing Director or **Department Head** and countersigned by the Group Accountant for payment up to £100, or in excess of £100 countersigned by **Finance Director** (or, in his absence, as delegated).

- Acceptance of Bills of Exchange – authorities are same as for cheque signing.

- **Forward Contracts:** For the protection of price of goods for resale placed by Finance Director. Otherwise by Finance Director with reference to CEO.

- **Transfer of Funds:** Same rules apply as for cheque signatories.

- **Finance Agreements:** Applications for capital expenditure should bear an addendum signed by the person authorised approving the expenditure, requesting, where necessary, that the Finance Director or Finance Controller arrange the appropriate HP or Leasing finance. Such agreements can only be signed by **CEO** or **Finance Director**.

Sealing of Documents

To be supported by a Company Minute and sealing of the document to be signed by Director of the Company and countersigned by Company Secretary.

6. COMPETENCIES FOR POTENTIAL SENIOR MANAGEMENT

Checked by using PPA & TEAM PLAYER ANALYSIS

- ### Intellectual Capability

  Candidates must exhibit clearly defined intellectual capability for the post considered and also for the one above. In younger people they should be considered for several posts above. Formal qualifications and reference *must* be checked.

- ### Strategic Thinking

  The ability to pick up trends and opportunities. Analytical thinking on its own is not enough.

  Relationship building: ensuring that business efforts are aligned with all stakeholders from shareholders to suppliers.

- ### Flexibility

  The ability to react to change and to new demands, rather than just sit a situation out.

- ### Interpersonal Understanding

  Reading people and situations and using this understanding to motivate staff.

- ### Group Management

  Focusing the team on its goals and providing it with a clear picture of the outcomes and processes needed to achieve goals.

- **Multicultural Sensitivity**

  Using differences to enrich business and business decisions. It means saying there is more than one way of doing something.

- **Co-operation**

  This is true team working when all involved in the winning result get their reward.

- **Past Employment**

  Must be acceptable. Not too many job changes or unexplained departures from a position.

In summary, when recruiting or promoting someone to a senior post, the following characteristics should be checked.

- **Technical knowledge;**
- **Effective communication;**
- **Teamwork;**
- **Setting high standards;**
- **Concern for accuracy;**
- **Taking initiative;**
- **Concern for effectiveness;**
- **Flexibility;**
- **Innovation.**

These characteristics should be investigated *in detail* by using **PPA and Team Player Analyses** and *no one* should be appointed if they do not display the required characteristics and competencies which must be decided *before* the advertising and interviewing process is carried out. Proper Job Specifications should be prepared before interview.

7. THE ROLE OF THE WORLDWIDE PRODUCT MANAGER

Title: PRODUCT MANAGER

Responsibility:

Reports to:

Supervises: All Subsidiaries

Job Requirements:

1. To become informed of all the relevant technologies and developments on a continuing basis.

2. To ensure the European Sales specialists are also fully informed.

3. To maintain existing technical links with suppliers and develop new ones as necessary.

4. To ensure that products at all times are technically competitive and yield a gross (adequate) margin to the sales companies.

5. To ensure that at each location there is a technically competent specialist to provide in-depth back-up support, advice and guidance to the field sales force.

6. To ensure good co-ordination and communication between the regions in placing business in the most advantageous way.

7. To advise on 'specials'; or custom designs to ensure they are technically sound and safely sourced.

8. To negotiate proper warranty conditions and check that each region understands them.

9. To ensure proper drawings and specifications are recorded and saved within the company.

To encourage technical 'awareness' throughout Europe.

8. THE ROLE OF A SALES MANAGER

A Sales Manager should have all the qualifications of a salesman and must have been a successful salesman. It does not follow that a successful salesman can become a Sales Manager but it is certain that an unsuccessful Salesman cannot become a Sales Manager.

A prime requirement of the job of the Sales Manager is to be very easily able to do the job of a salesman. Naturally, he must be technically qualified.

Sales Manager's tasks

A Sales Manager must be capable of understanding the nature of the company's business, its customers, and their geographical distribution.

He must be capable of interviewing, selecting, and hiring successful Salesmen. Having hired the potential salesman, he should ensure that he adequately trains them in the company's products and ethics and methods of the company.

He should employ salesmen so that they are efficiently deployed. This means that they must be located close to a good customer base and they must be shown how to plan a well thought-out calling pattern to maximise the time they spend in front of customers.

He must ensure that all products have an up-to-date data sheet, together with a short form catalogue of all products.

A Sales Manager must be capable, having deployed his sales force and trained them in an efficient manner of operation, of motivating them to a high degree so that they maximise their performance.

He should be constantly checking their performance, helping and motivating. Regular appraisal against objectives should be carried out and suitable action taken when performance falls below standards set.

He should devise a reporting system which enables the salesmen to easily record for the company the work which he has carried out.

He should further identify the large customers which would require a Sales Manager's personal attention. A Sales Manager must be capable of determining which level of business is pertinent to his personal intervention and ensure that all contracts above a certain size receive his personal attention.

Having achieved a properly deployed and efficient sales force with a good reporting system, the Sales Manager should ensure that there is a fully effective advertising PR and exhibition programme which will produce a continuous stream of new leads for the salesmen to follow.

He must have a system which ensures that all enquiries are properly followed up.

On top of these general duties, a Sales Manager should be capable of knowing the industry in which he is involved, that he can identify major potential customers without the need for an enquiry.

Finally, a Sales Manager must be capable of having sufficient knowledge of his business that he can provide the company with a reasonably accurate forecast of the expected order input for the following twelve-month period.

He must understand the company Objectives and Policies and ensure that they are fully followed by both himself and his staff.

His forward viewing horizon must be in the region of 6-12 months.

9. THE ROLE OF MANAGING DIRECTOR OF A SALES COMPANY

The role of Managing Director in a company is detailed below. This description gives clear guidelines with regard to responsibilities and obligations towards the Corporate Objectives and Policies. Particular reference is made to the appointment of an adequate Sales Manager whose role is detailed on a separate sheet.

The Managing Director of a technical sales company must first and foremost understand that he is running a technical sales company and ensure that it is an efficient one in all its different respects.

It is very desirable that he is a capable and efficient salesman but it is not necessary that he has been an efficient and capable Sales Manager, as the role of a Managing Director and Sales Manager are different.

The Managing Director is responsible for the total running of the company to meet the stated objectives of the company. The Managing Director is also responsible for ensuring that the Corporate Objectives are clearly understood by everybody and carried out to the letter.

Further, he must understand the policies laid down by the Board of Directors and ensure their successful implementation.

He must ensure that there is 20% per annum growth and 10% profit.

To do this he must ensure he employs adequate staff in all departments, particularly in the sales functions.

He must ensure that there is a growing and continuous source of new product and he must make certain that his Sales Manager is fully carrying out his responsibilities.

He must report his sales force with adequate and competent internal staff who are responsible for order processing, order delivery and finance.

He is responsible for the recruitment policies and the continuous training of all staff. He is responsible for ensuring that a proper staff appraisal system is in place and that his senior staff are well trained in the application of the system. He is further responsible for ensuring that proper attention is paid to matters of succession.

It is the responsibility of the Managing Director to understand all matters of discipline and to ensure that all his senior people understand the policies and how they should be implemented.

He must ensure that the company operates at its maximum efficiency and with maximum ambition at all times.

He should ensure that the financial policy is understood by all the relevant staff and that all financial matters are managed within the guidelines set down by the Board.

He must be aware of all significant and major customer situations and should be involved in any negotiations with major customers which require his level of expertise and judgement.

His forward viewing horizon must be on a 1-2 year time scale.

10. RECRUITMENT AND PEOPLE MANAGEMENT POLICIES

- The company has people management as a part of stated Corporate Objectives and Policies.

- For the purposes of explanation of these objectives and policies, directors and managers are personally responsible for the recruitment and retention of high-quality staff.

- All staff should be made aware of the whole group and its policies.

- Managers and directors are responsible for the positive motivation of the staff reporting to them. They are also responsible for their career development and training.

- They are further responsible for their general wellbeing. This means providing an environment which is stimulating and exciting. It is essential that managers understand that it is their duty to motivate and enthuse their junior staff and colleagues.

- This should be a conscious and full-time occupation and not something which is bolted on from time to time at motivating meetings.

- These policies will be pursued through individual appraisal carried out at least once a year, but at more regular intervals where it is felt to be beneficial.

- Recruitment and retention plus personal development is a major responsibility of all directors and will be part of their own appraisal.

11. REQUIREMENTS FOR MEMBERS OF THE MAIN BOARD

1. To fully understand and agree with the Corporate Objectives.

2. To implement them on a daily basis.

3. To understand and agree and implement the stated Company Policies and Strategies.

4. To understand the worldwide structure and the differing needs of each location.

5. To work closely and cooperatively with the Chairman.

6. To ensure all staff in direct contact are kept aware of international needs.

7. To visit worldwide locations regularly to know the businesses there and the staff.

8. To engender enthusiasm at all levels for staff.

12. GUIDELINES FOR TRADING COMPANIES

The rules which are detailed below are intended to be followed at all times. Deviation from them should be a matter of discussion between personnel at Managing Director level and Main Board Director level.

1. Gross Margin should ideally be 33% minimum.

2. Overhead costs must be controlled to be less than 20% sales unless the gross margin is higher than 33%. In this case the overhead can be increased in direct proportion to the increase in gross margin times 0.5.

3. Increases in overhead cannot be against projected sales but only against a minimum of a quarter's increase in shipments plus order cover at the same level for the following three months. That is, the money must be at least in a debtor's position before it is committed and future projections of orders received must be the same level.

4. Any expenditure above this must be regarded as investment and will require full main Board sanction.

5. Stock levels must be a maximum of approximately two months' of purchases; that is, the equivalent of one month of goods in transit plus a working stock of one month.

6. All inter-group debt must be settled on a 30-day basis.

7. All capital purchases must be pre-planned in the

budget. They can only be implemented if:

a) The sales and profits targets are being met, and,

b) The order is signed by one company director and one main Board Director.

8. All capital purchases **above £5,000** must be notified in advance to the Chairman.

9. The advertising, exhibitions, printing and salary budgets cannot be spent in advance of sales performance on an individual basis when compared to the planned budgets.

10. Authorisation levels are also applicable for the issue of Credit Notes.

11. Orders can only be accepted for a creditworthy customer. All credit checks and authorisation must be obtained before the order is placed on suppliers.

12. No commitment can be given to a supplier which is not fully passed on to the customer. That is, if we have not yet received a fully confirmed order and call-off schedule, we must not give one to the supplier.

13. Orders without scheduled call-offs must be separately identified in the reporting statistics.

In order to fulfil the requirements of the rules set out for trading companies regarding overhead structure, the following **'ideal'** overhead structure has been broken down as follows:

IDEAL OVERHEAD STRUCTURE FOR TRADING COMPANIES

Salaries	–	Direct
Salaries	–	Indirect
Factoring and		
Administration Charge		
Management Charge	–	Salaries

Other Staff Costs	
Total Staff	**10%**

Advertising	1.4
Exhibitions	0.5

Printing and Stationery	0.4
Postage	0.2
Telephone & Fax	0.5
Motor	0.4
Travel	0.8
Entertainment	0.05
D&D	0.5

Rent & Rates	0.5
Light & Heat	0.1
Repairs	0.2

Legal & Professional	0.2
Audit	0.4
Sundry	0.05
Training & Recruitment	0.4
Staff Welfare	0.1

Interest	
Depreciation	
Factors Discount Charge	
Management Charge – not salaries	
Bad debts	3.5

TOTAL	**20%**

13. TERMS AND CONDITIONS FOR CONTRACTUAL SALES

These Terms and Conditions must be applied to monthly call-off deliveries in order to qualify for quantity discounts.

1. Order must be firm for the whole amount of order to qualify for price required.
2. Delivery can be scheduled for a maximum of 12 months. Delivery dates and quantities for the total order are required with order.
3. Amendments to the delivery schedule can be made provided that 12 weeks' written notice is given and that the original term of the order is not exceeded.
4. The price is held firm only for 3 months at a time to be renegotiated to take account of inflationary elements or exchange differences.
5. The price is subject to the exchange rate at time of invoicing.
6. If the whole order is not taken, the price may be increased retrospectively to the price holding at the level of deliveries actually made.
7. Material specifically purchased for the order if not able to be disposed of elsewhere will be charged to the customer.
8. Payment terms are 30 days nett.

14. CONTRACT TERMS FOR SCHEDULED ORDERS

1. The Order must be **FIRM** for the whole quantity. Customer's credit rating must be adequate for the whole order.

2. The schedule must be realistic and regular (not for example 1,000 pcs, 10 now, and 990 TBA). A ramp-up period is acceptable but must not be more than 3 months.

3. Maximum period is 12 months but this can be extended to 14 months during the life of the order, if the customer has problems. *Beyond this the price will be variable.*

4. 80% of the quantity ***must*** be taken in a 12-month period even if the end date for the total quantity is extended as in 3.

5. The price must include currency protection or the customer understands they will have a variable price at the invoice date.

6. Variations in call-off can only be accepted with the following rules:

a) With ONE month's notice – **None**

b) With TWO months' notice – **10% change**

c) With THREE months' notice – **20% change**

d) With FOUR months' notice – **30% change**

The quantity changes are not cumulative, they only work against the original schedule, i.e. if 100 pcs per month placed. The minimum quantity in any month is 70 pcs (remember 80% must be taken in the scheduled period).

7. Cancellation is available but all materials purchased must be paid for plus overhead and administration costs.

All payments must be made on time. If delays are caused by non-payment beyond ONE month overdue, we may invoice all the order immediately at contract price.

15. RULES FOR MANUFACTURING COMPANIES

Gross Margin

a) Gross Margin should be sufficient to achieve a minimum profit (contribution) of 12% on sales.

Because of variations in the overhead structure of manufacturing companies, the overhead structure necessary to achieve the above will be agreed individually.

b) Direct costs included in cost of sales are:

Direct materials; direct labour and applicable on-costs.

c) When calculating cost of sales, appropriate adjustments should be made for stock movements.

d) If appropriate, a standard costing system to control direct material and labour costs should be employed.

Stocks

a) A suitable system of stock control should be employed to confirm the accuracy of valuation of raw materials, work in progress and finished goods. If a perpetual inventory system is employed and providing this gives accurate and fully documented results, then the full physical stock checks are not necessary. If such a system is not used then a full physical check must be carried out at least quarterly.

b) The valuation basis should be according to group policy i.e. at the lower of cost and net realisable value, where appropriate attributable costs may be included.

c) Materials should be used on a First In, First Out basis.

d) All purchases of production materials should be against booked customer orders; if the customer order is scheduled, material purchases should also be scheduled to match. Any terms and conditions imposed by the customer e.g. cancellation due to late delivery, must be passed on to the supplier. **All purchase orders must be in writing and properly authorised.**

e) Stock holdings must be minimised. A suitable level appropriate to the particular production process will be set for each company.

f) It is sometimes necessary to purchase production materials for stock e.g. where the material is used on a number of different manufactured parts. If this is the case, then stock and re-order levels must be carefully monitored to ensure that holdings are minimised.

Sales and Debtors

a) All quotations must be in writing and include our terms and conditions. Any quotation must be properly authorised and if over £100k or equivalent, must be notified to the Chairman.

b) All sales orders must be in writing, terms and conditions must be checked, and any areas of disagreement negotiated with the customer.

c) No order may be accepted from a customer who is not creditworthy and all appropriate checks must be carried out. This should be done prior to quotation for a new customer and also prior to delivery for **all** customers. Delivery should be withheld if a customer has exceeded his credit limit.

d) Debtors must be minimised, a suitable level will be set for each company.

Cash Flow

a) A detailed cash flow forecast should be maintained showing weekly income and expenditure for a minimum of 2 months into the future. Cash movements should be controlled to remain within this forecast on a net basis for at least the next 4 weeks. Any major departure **(≥£10k or equivalent)** from the forecast must be notified to Head Office immediately.

Design and Development

a) All proposed design and development projects must be checked for technical and financial viability prior to commencement by the appropriate Board.

b) All projects must be properly authorised and progress monitored carefully against a project timetable. Any project with costs that are likely to exceed £50k or equivalent must receive Board approval prior to commencement.

c) D&D projects that can be shown to have future

value may be capitalised according to the published group policy.

Capital Expenditure

a) All proposed capital expenditure should be included in the budget.

b) A capital expenditure justification should be prepared for all expenditure over £2,000 showing the reason for requiring the asset and the financial return. The pay-back period should not exceed 3 years.

c) Provided that the requirement was included in the capital budget, a payback of 3 years or less can be demonstrated and the company is meeting its objectives (see below), the asset may be purchased.

- **For all purchases over £10k the Finance Director must be consulted regarding finance.**

- **For all purchases over £25k the Chairman /Managing Director must be consulted for final approval.**

d) All non-budgeted capital expenditure over £1,000 must be referred to the Chairman/Managing Director for approval.

General

a) A return on capital invested should exceed other potential investments.

b) The trend of the business should be monitored at least every 3 months and appropriate action taken.

If growth is faster than previously experienced, then resources should be examined to check adequacy and, if necessary, a plan formulated to manage the increased growth. If this requires expenditure outside that budgeted, then the plan should be submitted to the company for discussion and approval.

Conversely, if the situation shows a decline in the company's position, a plan to restore the situation must be devised – this must be submitted to the company without delay and the plan implemented following approval. All capital expenditure, whether budgeted or not, must only be carried out with the company's approval and all overhead expenditure and cash payments reduced to a minimum.

c) Budgets must be prepared annually.

A full business review should also be carried out annually, preferably just before preparing the budget for the coming year.

16. MANUFACTURING UNITS IDEAL RATIOS FOR OVERHEAD

			% of total Revenue
SALES			**100.0**
COST OF FINISHED PRODUCT IN STORES			55.0
GROSS MARGIN			45.0
PRODUCTION COSTS	fixed		2.7
	variable		3.8
DISTRIBUTION			0.3
DEPRECIATION			1.0
DESIGN & DEVELOPMENT COSTS			1.5
SALES			4.1
ADMINISTRATION			1.3
FINANCIAL COSTS			3.3
STAFF	PRODUCTION	4.5	
	SALES	4.0	
	DESIGN & DEV	4.5	
	ADMIN	2.0	
			15.0
Overheads Total			33.0
CONTRIBUTION			12.0

NB: This set of ratios provides a general pattern for manufacturing companies, however, it should be noted that local circumstances, product type and volume will have a bearing and ratios should be modified to accommodate this.

17. SALES ACTIVITIES

In order to maximise sales at all times, the following guidelines should be used as a constant check list. The result of following these guidelines will be reflected in a well-run sales company.

In general, a twice yearly full audit of the items should ensure continuity of effort.

Current Products:

Full set of data sheets;

Regular PR and advertising;

Knowledge of customer base;

Knowledge of sales by product;

Sales dynamics (growth or death);

Competition;

Supplier capability.

Future Products:

A good plan of product introduction;

Preliminary data sheets;

Possible suppliers;

Methods of searching for new products with examples;

Market research.

Sales Staff:

Proper geographic coverage;

Highly daily call rate (3 to 4 minimum);

Knowledge of customers;

Good calling plan giving good coverage of existing customers with time to call on new ones;

Good reporting system;

Training programme;

Competition knowledge;

Following up leads from adverts and PR.

Sales Management:

Plan for this month's sales;

Plan for next month's sales;

Plan for next 6 months' sales;

Management of salesmen;

Advertising programme;

PR programme;

Major customer visits;

Monitoring salesmen's calls;

Monitoring of calls against leads;

Forecasting.

Advertising, PR, and Exhibitions:

Fully integrated plan promoting existing and future products costing about 2.5% of sales turnover dependent upon individual company market place. It should cover products individually as well as generic and have good company image.

18. LIST OF INFORMATION NEEDED FOR LARGER ENQUIRIES

Where we have identified, targeted, and obtained large enquiries from potential customers, the following information needs to be obtained prior to formal quotation.

Failure to address these issues from the beginning has been seen on many occasions to result in problems later on in the order/delivery/payment cycle.

1. Name of customer?
2. Who are they? Part of a larger company or independent?
3. Approximate size?
4. What do they make?
5. How old are they?
6. Product Details:

6a) **Existing Business**

i) Who is the current supplier?

ii) What is the reason for a change? (in detail)

iii) What is the current usage?

iv) What is the competition part number and specification?

6b) **New Business**

i)   What is the product the component will be used in?

ii) What is the length of message to be displayed and does it need graphics?

iii) What distance must it be read from and what angles?

iv) What is the temperature range, operating and storage?

v) Other environmental conditions – shock, vibration, altitude, humidity;

vi) Lighting conditions – does it need to be seen in daylight and night time?

vii) Lifetime requirement?

viii) Any colour requirements?

19. FINANCIAL ISSUES

1. TREASURY POLICIES

Four main areas of responsibility have been identified in defining the role of the Treasury function:

1. **The conservation of cash resources.**
2. **The financing of the company at the lowest overall cost.**
3. **The protection of the company from the adverse effects of foreign exchange rate fluctuations.**
4. **To ensure that adequate financial services are available for the smooth running of the organisation.**

The following report is directed particularly to item 2 and 3 above and is intended to establish policies and procedures which should be complied with.

It may be appropriate at this stage to state that the company clearly recognises that the various financial options available to protect against foreign exchange risk only offer short-term solutions at a highly visible cost, and that long-term earnings are ultimately a question of operating margin.

2. CURRENCY EXPOSURE POLICY

Objective:

To minimise exposure to foreign exchange risk by adopting hedging techniques.

Policy:

To minimise risk without any speculation in the various markets.

Method:

The responsibility for currency and exposure risk management will be vested in the Treasury Department.

The definition of permitted transactions and the authority levels of staff involved in these transactions will be as approved by the Executive Management.

3. STAFF PROCEDURES

1. To execute currency Spot and Forward transactions according to their authority limits and within the credit limits advised to each correspondent bank.

2. Identify matched and unmatched transactions as part of regular reporting requirements.

3. Prepare a hedging plan to protect the company from exposed transactions.

4. Undertake hedging transactions according to

authority and credit limits.

5. Ensure that hard currency liabilities and soft currency assets are regularly reviewed and as judged necessary covered in order to reduce the downside currency risk.

6. Report to the Treasurer all completed deals.

Review:

The Treasury Committee will meet on a weekly basis to review the current status of exposure risk and to consider future risk. The Committee's decisions and proposals will be minuted.

A Treasury report will be presented to the Main Board on a periodic basis.

Balance Sheet Exposure:

The company's funding is dispersed over several currencies including US Dollars, Euros and Yen and has been structure in such a manner that wherever possible, borrowings have been drawn down in currencies where either funding rates are low and/or interest costs can be fully absorbed.

The company policy will be to protect the Balance Sheet wherever hyperinflation exists. The definition of hyperinflation is wherever the local inflation rate exceeds 20%.

Method of Managing Exposure:

1. Maximise dividend remittances, the objective

being, where tax efficient, to remit a minimum of 2/3 of prior year after tax earnings.

2. Match borrowings against assets in exposed currencies.

3. Local management will maximise liquidity and convert available funds into a hard currency as agreed with Treasury.

Profit and Loss Exposure:

All companies will maintain a policy of increasing prices at a minimum in line with inflation and reducing operating costs to maintain growth in earnings.

Transaction Exposure:

The company philosophy towards operating exposure management is active as opposed to passive. Operating exposures are seen as a cost of doing business and as such they must be managed efficiently if the company is to retain a competitive advantage.

Operating exposures are defined to include both existing booked foreign currency receivables and payables and future foreign currency flows which are either committed or can be forecast with some certainty.

The company policy will be to reduce exposure selectively according to the level of risk perceived and the attendant costs involved.

Procedure:

1. Identify exposure positions.

2. Assess the risk associated with the position. Risk will be measured against the magnitude of the long- or short-term position in a currency and the likely strength or weakness of the currency involved.

3. Decide within Board parameters which potential impacts are unacceptable.

4. Reduce unacceptable exposure positions through the most cost effective hedging techniques.

Protection will be effected by the use of:

Forward currency contracts/options;

Foreign currency accounts;

Currency of billing/payment;

Leading/lagging of third party and inter-company foreign currency payables;

Price adjustments;

Cash management improvements.

Currently the majority of the company's transaction exposure is in short positions held by subsidiary operations on their trading account with the major source companies. These positions can be controlled through the company by either leading or lagging inter-company settlements or by local cover carried out by the local management.

Source company transactions are currently billed in

the currency of the source company.

The current procedure is for inter-company borrowings and other foreign currency transactions to be reviewed at Headquarter level and direction given to local companies as to the action to be taken to provide cover. Cover will be limited to known liabilities for goods or services supplied.

In order to keep the Finance Committee of the Board informed of the levels of risk involved, it is proposed that the Committee will be informed in the following circumstances:

If the exposure to exchange risk were to be greater than £50k in any exposed currency, such risk would be referred to the Finance Committee.

Borrowings and Interest Rates:

The main borrowing currencies will be in £ Sterling, US$, and Japanese Yen.

Overseas Borrowing:

Borrowing by overseas companies will be managed by the Treasurer and in the appropriate circumstances referred to the Finance Committee.

a) Borrowing will be arranged where required, but will always be matched by assets in the local currency.

b) Any borrowings in excess of £25k in any overseas company will be referred to the Finance Committee.

The Treasurer will reduce Balance Sheet exposure by moving funds into non-exposed currencies – primarily £ Sterling.

4. CURRENCY EXPOSURE MANAGEMENT

The impact on the company of foreign exchange movements arises in two ways. The first is from transactions done and committed in foreign currencies. The second arises from the translation of the currency Balance Sheets of foreign subsidiaries. These two types of risk are often referred to by analysts as 'cash flow risk' and 'balance sheet risk' or sometimes as 'transaction risk' and 'translation risk'.

The approach to both issues takes the same form:

1. **Identify exposure positions:**

The following require to be identified:

a) Foreign currency receivables/payables which have been booked;

b) Foreign currency transaction flows which are either already committed to or can be forecast with some certainty;

c) All dividend, royalty, and management charges payments;

d) Foreign currency financial flows, e.g. interest and principal payments;

e) Any other commercial or financial funds flow transacted in a foreign currency.

This identification process will require to look forward over a reasonable time span – at a minimum on a 3-month basis in some detail and ideally, even if in very broad terms, a view should also be taken from time to time on a twelve month perspective.

2. **Assessment of Risk:**

A decision to hedge a risk has to be made in the context of the potential cost/risk perceived. It is necessary to make a judgement on future market trends. To make no projection implicitly assumes that exchange rates will not change – in itself a forecast.

It is necessary to calculate for each exposed transaction:

Exposure Position x Projected Exchange Rate Change = Expected Gain/Loss

---

The projected exchange rate can be based on personal judgement and/or analysts' reviews. For major exposures a range of projections should be made together with a view on the likelihood of each outcome. This may result in a very low expectation of loss but at the same time, due to size of the overall exposure, the possibility of a loss which, if realised, could be significant. It is important to review a whole range of possible outcomes and therefore impacts.

3. **Decide which impacts are unacceptable:**

Clearly any loss is unwanted but hedging involves cost. The automatic elimination of all transaction risk could require substantial unnecessary costs. Acceptable risk thresholds have to be established.

A company's philosophy towards operating exposure management should be active as opposed to passive. Operating exposures are seen as a cost of doing business and as such they must be managed efficiently if the company is to retain a competitive advantage. Company policy is to reduce exposure selectively according to the level of risk perceived and the attendant costs involved. Currently the Board has agreed that exposures in any one currency up to £25k may be managed by senior staff. For exposures of a larger amount, proposed hedging strategies require to be submitted to the Board.

4. **Risk Limitation:**

Protection will be effected by the use of:

Forward currency instruments;

Foreign currency accounts;

Adjustments to the currency of billing/payment;

Leading/lagging of third party and inter-company foreign currency payables;

Price adjustments;

Cash management improvements.

5. **Balance Sheet Risk:**

Following the approach identified above, it is first necessary to identify the exposure involved. The extent of this exposure can be seen as the value of the equity investment in the subsidiary. In assessing the risk involved in this exposure, the company's position is that their investment in its overseas subsidiaries are long-term commitments. There is an assumption in the case of fixed assets that over the life of the investment inflation differentials will be compensated by equivalent exchange rate movements. If appropriate, opportunities will be taken on a selective basis to limit exposure by direct matching. The company, however, will not enter into forward exchange transactions as a method of reducing translation exposure.

The company's approach in limiting its Balance Sheet exposure will be confined to the following methods:

1. Maximum use will be made of local borrowings when financing subsidiaries. Loans from the parent company will be avoided if at all possible.
2. Dividend remittances will be maximised. If required, use will be made of local borrowings to finance dividend payments.
3. Excess liquidity will either be converted into a hard currency or will be invested at rates of return at least equivalent to the local currency devaluation.

In undertaking these approaches to translation

management, remembering that adverse currency movements can eliminate apparent savings on interest rates, attention will be paid to the interest cost involved as compared to the currency risk and also to the tax implications for both the company involved and the Group as a whole.

Long-Term Exposure:

In addressing long-term exposures to depreciating currencies, Treasury management has to demonstrate to operating management the various financial options available to protect against foreign exchange risk. It must be understood that these only offer short-term solutions at a highly visible cost, and that long-term earnings are ultimately a question operating margins.

5. CREDIT EXPOSURE

The definition of Credit Exposure is the total exposure to risk arising from the period during which we are *required* to take delivery of goods which have been ordered, and during which there is any chance of our not being paid for them.

For example:

If a Purchase Order can be cancelled, provided (say) 3 months' notice is given, then our exposure here is 3 months' purchases.

If the same order is sold with 60-day payment terms, then the total risk exposure is 5 months – 3 months on the Order and 2 months Credit Exposure on sales. If the sale is factored without recourse, then there is no sales credit risk and the total exposure is only 3 months.

The Board has agreed that before quoting or accepting any large sales orders, the Finance Director is to be advised if the total exposure is over £100k (or equivalent). Thus, in the above examples, with 60-day sales credit terms, an order worth £20k/month exceeds this limit, while an order which is fully factored only exceeds the limit at £33k/month (in each case assuming that the non-cancellable period of the purchase order is 3 months).

ADDENDUM 2

SOME IDEAS ON SELLING

SELLING DIRECT TO OTHER COMPANIES

INDEX

1. Product Knowledge: Essential
2. Sales Area Knowledge
3. Company Knowledge
4. Organisation of Selling
5. In front of Customer (Intangible benefits)
6. Exploitation of Existing Customers
7. Exploitation of Contact within Organisation
8. Follow-up (quotations, literature)
9. Reference Selling
10. Creating Targets

1. PRODUCT KNOWLEDGE FOR SALES STAFF

Product knowledge is vital to effective selling. However, it is only important to know the main advantages of your product.

If it gets too technical, refer back to Technical Support Staff.

Remember **FAB (Features, Advantages, Benefits)**

> ## DO NOT SELL WHAT YOU HAVE GOT, BUT SELL WHAT YOU CAN 'DO'.

2. SALES AREA KNOWLEDGE

BE AWARE OF NEW POTENTIAL. You should know all the existing and potential customers in your area.

Read magazine adverts, read directories, ask at existing customers. Check all new enquiries.

If you cannot remember all of your area in detail, make certain you have a system which will cope.

All significant people in existing customers should be on a company file and in your own private system if you need it.

You should have maps marked with all customer locations, to help plan your travelling to be efficient.

> ## BE AWARE OF NEW POTENTIAL.

3. COMPANY KNOWLEDGE

Be certain you really know *your* own company's position.

Terms of Trading

Contractual Terms

Payment Terms

Policy on Returns

Who to refer to with problems

Warranty Period

Service given

KNOW YOUR LITERATURE

Your two differing roles

A. In your customer's company you represent the whole of your company at all times.

B. Inside your company, you represent the *customer's* interests.

BE CONFIDENT BUT NOT ARROGANT

BE PRO-ACTIVE BUT ENSURE YOU ENCOURAGE THE CUSTOMER TO TALK.

---

4. HOW TO ORGANISE A SALESPERSON'S WORKING DAY

This is the *single most important component in successful selling*.

A majority of your time can be wasted in travelling. It is essential to reduce this to a minimum. This can only be done by organised, well thought-out planning of journeys and calls.

a) Suns and Satellites

Treat major customers as Suns and smaller companies as Satellite calls. Do the small calls on the way to, in between or returning from, major calls at Suns.

b) Travel to your furthest distance in the morning and work backwards towards your base.

c) Make certain that the maximum number of people are seen on every call.

Remember there are many groups of people who influence buying decisions, e.g. Engineers, Production, Q.A. Buyers. They should all be involved in your calling cycle, particularly on large orders.

DO NOT ignore any one of them, even if it is just to say hello.

d) Try to do one new or cold call every day.

e) Review what you are going to talk about before going into the company. Two minutes sitting in the car reviewing the last call and planning objectives of new calls vastly increases effectiveness.

f) Have all literature with you in pre-prepared packs.

g) Plan time of calling cycles based upon turnover (actual and potential).

h) Exploit existing customers most.

i) You can generally sell more to bigger customers.

KNOW WHAT YOU ARE DOING AND WHY YOU ARE DOING IT.

5. IN FRONT OF A CUSTOMER

Be smart;

Be knowledgeable;

Be confident;

Be interested and inquisitive;

Listen twice as much as talk. You have two ears and only one mouth;

Be organised;

Listen to the customer's *needs*.

Unconscious incompetent, conscious incompetent, conscious competent; unconscious competent.

There are 4 stages of competency.

In explanation, think of a baby and shoes. A baby who can't put shoes on and doesn't know it wants to is *unconsciously incompetent*. Then the baby understands shoes but cannot put them on, and is *consciously incompetent*. Next, it understands about putting shoes on and can do it but has to think about it, *consciously competent*. Finally, the baby puts them on without thinking and has become *unconsciously competent*.

You will follow this process in selling. BUT, the highest level when you are *unconsciously competent* is to be 'aware' so that if something is going wrong you can switch back into *consciously competent* and sort out any problems that have arisen.

ALWAYS LOOK FOR NEW BUSINESS AFTER SECURING EXISTING BUSINESS.

---

6. EXPLOITATION OF EXISTING CUSTOMERS

It is vital to exploit every possible potential in existing customers before chasing after new ones.

It is efficient on your time and helps the company, e.g. only one set of accounts to reduce postage bills, etc.

Get to know other departments, other engineers, get to know about new projects. Find out the volume of purchasing, try to get a bigger share of the business.

DO NOT ASSUME THAT YOUR CUSTOMERS KNOW ALL ABOUT YOU OR YOUR PRODUCTS.

---

7. EXPLOITATION OF A CONTACT WITHIN A COMPANY

Most people are flattered by a *genuine* interest in their company and will be keen to display their knowledge. This particularly applies to standards and Q.A. engineers. Buyers in general tend to resent further intrusions into the company structure. Exploit this situation; try to get the existing contact to introduce you, it puts an obligation on the new contact to listen. Don't be put off by a buyer but don't fight it. Get around the company on another visit.

DON'T BE AFRAID TO ASK QUESTIONS AND GIVE PRAISE, BUT DON'T BE FALSE.

---

8. FOLLOW-UP QUOTATIONS AND LITERATURE REQUESTS

It is essential, wherever possible, to send quotations. It is also essential to follow them up.

Literature requests should all be vetted and interesting ones followed up even if only by telephone.

DON'T LEAVE UNFINISHED BUSINESS.

---

9. REFERENCE SELLING

Reference selling is the most powerful tool in the box. Always know someone else who has used the product successfully. Proffer these names and try to see they are well known.

Be very careful not to reveal secrets between competitors during a sales visit.

Some humour is very useful.

Try to arrange to have new customers contact existing ones for references (if it is *safe* to do so).

KNOW YOUR CUSTOMERS

Check their websites, Tweets, Facebook, LinkedIn, etc.

---

10. CREATING TARGETS. SET TARGETS AND MEET THEM

Set targets of calls per day.

Set targets for new customers secured per month.

Set targets of new contacts within customers.

Set targets of increased business with existing customers.

Set targets for new products discussed.

Tend only to talk about 3 items per visit, any more becomes confusing.

IF YOU DON'T MEET YOUR TARGETS, YOU ARE NOT TRYING.

IF YOU EXCEED YOUR TARGETS, THEY WERE TOO EASY.

SET TARGETS AND MEET THEM.

---

11. ONLINE AND INDIRECT SELLING

1. Website
2. Advertising
3. Mail Shots
4. Press Release (Products)
5. Press Release (Company)
6. Literature
7. Company Presentation

8. Gifts
9. Entertaining
10. Consistency

Advertising

It is important to decide the purpose of the adverts, e.g. tell about new product, improve image of company, seek replies, frighten competition, etc.

Once this is decided, the message should be very clear and simple.

Most adverts are product adverts. They should say:

a) What the product is;

b) What it does;

c) What its advantages are.

Remember price is a very potent message. If it's possible and relevant, mention it.

For product advertising, size has not been shown to correlate with number of replies, whereas location often does.

Mail Shots

Tend to be very expensive but if the message is specific, can be very powerful. Sometimes no other way will reach full potential.

Mailing lists can be bought reasonably economically. The costs come in the printing and posting.

The same goes for 'fold-ins', etc.

Don't forget the mailing cards system. This has

worked very well at lower costs.

Press Release for Products

This should be a number one activity in every company. They are free adverts and give bigger response than advertising.

They should:

a) Have bold ideas;

b) The body text should be in short specific sentences that are east to edit. 3 line spacing;

c) Make the message very clear;

d) Try to get on one page;

e) Try to get an interesting photograph;

f) Make certain it is typed nicely.

SEND AT LEAST ONE A MONTH TO ALL RELEVANT MEDIA.

Company Press Releases

Same rules as for product press releases. Can be very useful as company grows to enhance implied benefits of products. These should be much less frequent than product releases.

Product Information/Online/Websites etc.

Be generous with product information in quantity and even print it cheaply to enable it to be given away in bulk.

If it is possible economically, make it very smart.

Always make it informative and useful.

Remember, literature is a continuous salesman and must carry a proper.

SALES MESSAGE

1. FEATURES

2. ADVANTAGES

3. BENEFITS

Company Presentation

Do not hesitate to talk about your company. Bring out its good points.

Admit any bad ones but offset with good ones. Try to change bad features internally.

Be positive and proud of the company and its achievements.

Do not be shy about being a small company. Point out benefits.

Invite visitors to company when appropriate.

Telephone

The telephone is vital for making appointments, doing quick follow-ups to enquiries, and quotes. Always plan your calls out first both for time and purpose.

DO NOT LET TELEPHONE CALLS REPLACE VISITS.

Make certain that the people who primarily answer the telephone know what they are doing. They should know the company, products, and people and their jobs.

Do not bounce people around the company. If necessary, take their name and call them back.

Always sound friendly and helpful.

Make everyone in the company aware of the importance of the telephone.

Gifts

Gifts are unnecessary in 99% of all cases and cause more trouble than they are worth.

Entertaining

Restrict it to the absolute minimum. If you do wish to give a good lunch for a good or special order, make certain it is properly done.

Do not get drunk yourself.

Consistency

Make certain that all facets of the sales effort, both direct and indirect, are consistent with each other for objectives, quality, presentation, colour, etc.

Selling – Exhibitions

Exhibition stands should be large enough to attract attention but should look busy. New products should be prominently displayed.

Literature should be available but not taken away in volume.

Staff should know exactly what it is all about.

It pays to advertise your stand before the exhibition starts.

Invitations can obligate people to visit you. Keep a stand bright and clean at all times.

Exhibitions can have very heavy hidden expenditure.

YOUR WEBSITE IS VITAL BUT YOU MUST FIND WAYS TO ATTRACT POTENTIAL CUSTOMERS TO VISIT IT.

I hope that this book proves of some material value in your quest for growth. As indicated at the beginning it is not a magic formula but a collection of ideas which have proved themselves to be effective in a wide variety of companies around the world.

If you check on my activities with Densitron you will discover that I was ousted by a city investor who saw more value in a sports field we owned rather than the company's survival and progress. As far as I could follow it,his board abandoned the bulk of the things that made Densitron successful and concentrated on a less technical narrower range of products. Further they seemed to manage by a command and control method rather than managing by objectives.

They lost money in large amounts and many talented engineers and managers left to start their own companies. One comment I heard was that there was virtually nobody on the board who was technical and able to understand the company.

Over the following 14 years several of these start-ups grew to be more successful than the remaining remnants of Densitron. The final outcome has been, that late in 2015 one of these new companies bought what remained of Densitron for around one third of the value it floated at in 1986 29 years earlier. I congratulate them as I am confident that they will make it successful once again.

This final example indicates the power of the contents of this book. You should not just copy these ideas but use them in conjunction with your own talents to create your own success.